.

KENT STATE UNIVERSITY ATHLETICS

Kent State University's current intercollegiate athletics logo combines the university's mascot, the golden eagle, with the school's longtime nickname, the Golden Flashes, as symbolized through a golden lightning bolt. In 1925, the university's official colors were designated as blue and gold. (Courtesy of Kent State University Intercollegiate Athletics.)

On the front cover: Steve Stone pitched for the Golden Flashes in the late 1960s opposite catcher Thurman Munson. Both would go on to successful major-league careers. (Courtesy of the Kent State University Photographs Collections.)

On the back cover: The women's gymnastics team celebrates another victory in a long history of achievement since its establishment in 1959. (Courtesy of the Kent State University Photographs Collections.)

Cover background: Coach Joseph Begala, pictured with his 1931 wrestling team, went on to become one of the most successful coaches in Kent State history. (Courtesy of the Kent State University Photographs Collections.)

KENT STATE UNIVERSITY ATHLETICS

Cara Gilgenbach and Theresa Walton

ARCADIA
PUBLISHING

Copyright © 2008 by Cara Gilgenbach and Theresa Walton
ISBN 978-1-5316-3227-4

Published by Arcadia Publishing
Charleston SC, Chicago IL, Portsmouth NH, San Francisco CA

Library of Congress Catalog Card Number: 2007936590

For all general information contact Arcadia Publishing at:
Telephone 843-853-2070
Fax 843-853-0044
E-mail sales@arcadiapublishing.com
For customer service and orders:
Toll-Free 1-888-313-2665

Visit us on the Internet at www.arcadiapublishing.com

CONTENTS

ACKNOWLEDGMENTS

The authors gratefully acknowledge the support and assistance of the following offices and individuals at Kent State University (KSU): Libraries and Media Services; Intercollegiate Athletics and Athletic Communications; the School of Exercise, Leisure and Sport; the photography unit of University Communications and Marketing; Alumni Relations; Laing Kennedy (director of Intercollegiate Athletics); Mark Weber (dean of Libraries and Media Services); Rose Fathauer (former Sports Information historian); Alan Ashby (Athletic Communications director); Matthew Lofton (Athletic Communications graduate student assistant); Gary Harwood (university photographer); and Nancy Schiappa (associate director of Alumni Relations). Thanks are due to KSU alumni Jan Valenti, who supplied very helpful information on women's sports in the 1960s, and Jeff Kurtz, who offered helpful suggestions on the final manuscript. Also appreciated is the work of Arcadia Publishing editor Jeff Ruetsche, who provided guidance and clarification throughout the planning and preparation of this text. Very special thanks are extended to production assistant Michael Hrusch.

INTRODUCTION

Kent State University (KSU), established as Kent State Normal School in 1910 by the State of Ohio as one of two northern Ohio normal schools, was charged with training teachers throughout the northeast region. Kent State functioned as a multicampus institution from its earliest days. During its first two years, before land clearing and construction of facilities on the Kent campus site, classes were offered in a number of locations in the area. Finally in the fall of 1913, the Kent campus was up and running.

Plans to expand the curriculum and programs to those of a large university offering advanced degrees began as early as 1915, reflected in the school's name change to Kent State Normal College, showing significant growth in just a few years. The State of Ohio formally conferred university status to the institution in 1935, realizing the vision of Kent's first president, John Edward McGilvrey. During the 1960s, the university established its first doctoral programs, including one in exercise physiology, and the institution began to distinguish itself as a key research university within the region. By the end of that same decade, a still existent eight-campus system was also in place.

KSU has enjoyed a storied athletic history that remains widely unknown, despite the fact that many outstanding professional athletes, Olympic athletes, and coaches are part of that history. Athletic activities were important elements of campus life from the earliest years of the school's existence. In 1914, students formed the athletic association, an organization that held a central place in campus life through the middle of the 20th century. In that same year, the school established its first intercollegiate athletic team—men's baseball.

From 1910 through the 1930s, the institution's administration placed less emphasis on intercollegiate athletics and instead focused on sports as related to physical education, teacher preparation, and student recreation. In keeping with national concerns over Americans' fitness, McGilvrey made membership in the athletic association and intramural sport compulsory for all students in 1917 with a focus on inclusive participation. Nonetheless, the arrival of KSU athletics legend Joseph Begala, who coached six athletic teams, and the appointment of George Donald Starn as head football coach and director of varsity athletics shortly thereafter signaled an increased focus and interest in intercollegiate sports.

As male enrollment dropped during the World War II years, the Women's Athletic Association enjoyed a resurgence of popularity. During this time, the linkage between athletic fitness and national defense came again to the fore. Building of new and expanded facilities, planned for many years but delayed by the uncertainty of war, regained attention in 1950 with the dedication of both a modern gymnasium and a new stadium.

The second half of the century brought increased concentration on intercollegiate athletics and less concern with the connection of sports to physical education, with athletics becoming a separate administrative unit. A number of distinguished coaches, athletes, and teams emerged, including Joseph Begala's nationally recognized wrestlers; internationally renown husband-and-wife gymnastics coaches Rudy and Janet Bachna; football coach Don James, who led Kent to its last bowl game in 1972; famed University of Notre Dame coach and KSU linebacker Lou Holtz; KSU's first sub-four-minute miler Sam Bair; basketball and tennis star Bonnie Beachy, who became Kent's all-time leading scorer in basketball; and numerous Olympic athletes such as Pete George, Marie (Walther) Bilski, Gerald Tinker, Thomas Jefferson, and Kim Kreiner.

The university became the focus of international attention when, on May 4, 1970, Ohio National Guard soldiers shot 13 students, 4 of them fatally, at an antiwar rally on the campus commons. As in the past, the administration targeted student involvement in athletics as part of a strategy for student campus participation other than political protest. As part of the process of recovering from May 4, KSU reinvigorated its intramural sports programs and enjoyed its greatest success in football with a trip to the Tangerine Bowl led by future Pro Football Hall of Fame inductee Jack Lambert. Along with Lambert, many Golden Flashes went on to professional athletics careers, such as the late New York Yankee Thurman Munson, his teammate Steve Stone, football player Don Nottingham, and British Open champion Ben Curtis.

Although long involved in athletic activities, female students did not gain significant support in intercollegiate competition until several years after the passage of national Title IX legislation. In the 1980s, 1990s, and into the present decade, women distinguished themselves in a number of individual and team sports, including basketball, field hockey, softball, and gymnastics. The Golden Flashes won the Jacoby Award for on-field excellence in women's athletics more times (six) than any other school in the Mid-American Conference (MAC), placing in the top three since 1996.

Several sports, including men's and women's golf, indoor and outdoor track, baseball, women's gymnastics, and men's and women's basketball, achieved excellence in the 21st century. Enthusiasm for KSU sports reached a high point in 2002 when the men's basketball team made an NCAA Elite Eight appearance. Within the highly competitive and costly Division I environment, KSU continues to face the challenge of maintaining elite athletic programs while also sustaining an academic focus. In recent years, KSU made a number of facilities improvements, funded in part through private donations, including renovations to the softball and baseball fields, installation of a new baseball stadium along with new field hockey and soccer fields, and the creation of a state-of-the-art golf training facility.

This book highlights selected moments, stories, and figures in KSU athletic history. Unfortunately, not every distinguished athlete, team, and faculty or staff member who contributed to the development of athletics could be included. Unless otherwise noted, all photographs in this book come from the university archives and university photographs collections. The availability and quality of images as well as the extent to which a subject helped to encapsulate the trends and key events within a given decade guided selections. Graduation years for individuals were provided when available. The absence of this notation does not necessarily indicate that individuals did not graduate. Due to space constraints, it was impossible to identify each individual in a given photograph. All the university's athletes and fans can take comfort, however, in the preservation of the extensive athletics records archived in the Departments of Special Collections and Archives and Intercollegiate Athletics. As KSU nears the marking of its centennial, the authors hope that this history honors the efforts and accomplishments of all the athletes, coaches, faculty, staff members, and fans who have shaped athletics at Kent for the past 100 years.

1

NORMAL SCHOOL AND

PHYSICAL EDUCATION

1910—1919

The mission of Kent State during the normal school era was to produce professionally trained teachers to meet the growing demands for elementary and high school educators. Athletic activities in this period primarily emphasized intramurals and sports as connected to the physical education curriculum. In the *Summer School Announcement of 1914*, physical education appeared for the first time as a separate department, although in previous years, courses of physical education could be found within the various courses of study.

Intramural play was first organized when the athletic association (for both "girls" and "boys") was founded in the winter term of 1914. Women organized themselves into four competing basketball squads, while the men formed baseball and basketball teams. Before the rise of intercollegiate athletics at Kent in the 1930s, intramural and club sports were the primary venues for athletic competition on campus. Intramurals were enthusiastically embraced by female students, who far outnumbered their male peers at this time, and a variety of individual and team sports were organized, including tennis, indoor baseball, horseshoes, swimming, table tennis, badminton, archery, bowling, handball, and soccer.

In keeping with national trends whereby physical education transitioned from the exercise-based gymnastics movement to a more sport-based methodology grounded in play theory, 1914 was also the year when Kent's first intercollegiate athletic team was established—men's baseball, coached by school custodian Alexander Whyte. Intercollegiate basketball competition premiered in 1915 sans coaching staff. Although attempts were made as early as 1915 to form a men's varsity football team, it would not be until the start of the next decade that a remotely viable team was in place.

Pres. John Edward McGilvrey, who had little interest at this time in varsity athletics but who viewed intramural play as integral to "national fitness," made participation in intramurals and membership in the athletic association compulsory for all students, starting in 1917. As the second decade of the 20th century came to a close, steadily increasing student enrollment and an as-yet modest physical plant made the lack of suitable athletic facilities at Kent a topic of great concern in the coming decade.

Women's intramural sport participation met with approval and encouragement. Posed on the steps of Merrill Hall, the first building constructed on campus, are members of two of the four basketball teams first organized by the athletic association in the winter of 1914. The acceptance of bloomers as athletic dress greatly enhanced these ball players' freedom of movement. While women across the country played basketball since the game was invented by James Naismith in 1891, in keeping with beliefs of women's weakness and frailty, these basketball players played by modified six-on-six rules, limiting each player to half court play and only three dribbles of the ball.

Coach Alexander Whyte led the Normal Nine, Kent State's first intercollegiate athletic team, pictured here in front of Merrill Hall (1914). Competing against other colleges, high schools, and industrial teams, the Normal Nine joined the growing arena of intercollegiate sport. Pres. John Edward McGilvrey favored recreational sport over varsity athletics, but coach Whyte drew on the popularity of baseball to create competitive opportunities for these men to participate in the national pastime.

Kent's first varsity basketball team played within the local area starting in 1914, competing against high school and other local teams. On January 22, 1915, the team faced its first collegiate opponent in a match against Otterbein College, played at home in the auditorium building atrium. The result was a resounding defeat of 56-5, but as the yearbook exclaimed, hopes were high to "win for Kent Normal a name in the basketball world."

In 1917, Pres. John Edward McGilvrey made compulsory membership in the athletic association as well as participation in intramural sports activities. He had little interest in varsity or intercollegiate athletics, and his interest in intramural sports was primarily in their connection to teacher training curricula. His attitude toward athletics would change over time, particularly in response to World War I.

Kent's first head of physical education was Ruth V. Atkinson. A graduate of the University of Chicago, University of Wisconsin, and Cornell, she was appointed at Kent in 1913 and was responsible for direction of the physical education department as well as most athletic activities for women. The curriculum then was focused on "school hygiene . . . [and] the means for promoting proper physical growth and development" as the course of study then indicated.

A physical education club was organized as early as 1917 and provided leadership for intramural activities, along with the athletic association. An indoor baseball league comprised of both student and faculty teams was formed. Basketball remained a popular choice, with teams being formed by dormitory mates, such as these Lowry Hall players (above), as well as along departmental lines, such as the domestic science team (below). Other teams of this era included the Live Wires, All Stars, and the Off Campus squad, as well as class teams. The 1920s would feature such whimsically named outfits as the Yankees, Rebels, Red Terrors, Lucky Strikes, Whippets, Patriots, Scarlets, Blockheads, and even the Flying Elephants.

Kent State's influence permeated the region. Many of its teachers were graduates of the school or participants in its extension program. This program, offered in over 20 cities and towns throughout northeast Ohio since 1912, allowed currently practicing teachers to work under the guidance of a Kent State faculty member to complete coursework. This system allowed teachers to earn two- or four-year normal school diplomas while working full-time. Many Kent-educated teachers would have directed the athletic activities of their respective schools. Kent State Normal School students also interacted with local schools through early athletic competitions against high school and industrial teams. In addition, area students were invited to campus for Play Days that included athletic competitions, along with social mixers and dances. Shown here are the boys' baseball and girls' basketball teams of the neighboring Ravenna Township High School.

Since 1914, Kent State operated a training school on campus that eventually enrolled students in grades kindergarten through 12 and provided teachers in training with real-life classroom experience. The University School, as it later became known, was fully integrated into campus life and assembled athletic teams of its own from as early as 1915. Pictured here are members of the Kent State High School's 1915 boys' baseball team and 1919 girls' basketball team. The school was housed in various physical locations through the years, first in Kent Hall, then Franklin Hall (originally named the William A. Cluff Teacher-Training Building), and eventually in the current Michael Schwartz building where it remained until its dissolution in 1982.

PHYSICAL EDUCATION

D.Powell

The American Physical Education Association formed the National Committee on Women's Sport in 1917. The philosophy of leaders in women's physical education can be summed up with the prevailing slogan "a girl for every sport, a sport for every girl." Women participated in a wide variety of activities that emphasized civic and physical development through physical education and recreational sports over competition.

University of Wisconsin graduate Marie Hyde Apple came to Kent State in 1918, when she was appointed as the school's third director of physical education for women. Throughout her 35-year career, she provided leadership for physical education as well as its attendant intramural program. A residence hall was dedicated in her honor in 1969.

2

S P O R T   F O R

N A T I O N A L   F I T N E S S

1 9 2 0 – 1 9 2 9

The experiences of World War I had cemented a growing concern with the physical fitness of America's youth as tied to national defense readiness. In 1924, the State of Ohio General Assembly created a mandatory system of health and physical education within the state's public schools, and Pres. John Edward McGilvrey responded by forming a new school of physical and health education and athletic coaching, with Arville O. DeWeese, M.D., brought in as its head. Having medical training was common for physical educators at this time, reflecting the strong health orientation of the field during this period.

Another major shift in physical education during this time was the focus on social development objectives with the adoption of play theory, which suggested that important aspects of human development were the social, physical, and intellectual skills learned during child's play. Thus sport came to take on an even more prominent role in physical education departments and teacher education programs.

In line with the national growth of collegiate sport, 1924 was an important year for athletics at Kent State. The *Chestnut Burr* yearbook remarked on the two new developments that marked the year: "With 1924 a new epoch in the glorious history of our college is to start. A new gymnasium, second to none in Ohio, will be ready for use and a new course—four years in Physical Training and Health Education leading to a degree—will be offered. A special faculty will be employed for this course and eventually a group of several hundred students will be enrolled."

While intramural sports still dominated the athletic scene, men's varsity athletics were on the cusp of gaining more prominence within campus life. Two events were bookends for the decade: 1920 finally saw the creation of a football squad, and in 1929, Kent State Normal College was admitted into the Ohio Athletic Conference.

Demonstrating the growing social aspects of sport, athletic traditions, such as a fall football homecoming event and the appearance of the normal college field band at games, also emerged in the 1920s.

Perhaps slowed by school president John Edward McGilvrey's disdain for competitive athletics and certainly due in some part to low male enrollment figures, Kent did not join the national trend of sponsoring football until 1920. With only a handful of men enrolled on campus that season, nearly all were members of this first team, which played only two games. Coached by the head of the education department, Prof. Paul G. Chandler (above, back right), the football team would not log a touchdown in the record books until 1923, and it was not until 1925 that a Kent football team won a game. Coach Chandler and some members of the team (below) returned to campus in recognition of the team's 50th anniversary and were honored at the September 26, 1970, football game against the State University of New York at Buffalo.

The first mascot name used by Kent State Normal School was the Kent State Silver Foxes, in homage to McGilvrey, who owned a silver fox ranch adjacent to campus. The name first appeared during the 1923 school year. The school annual of that same year notes the ranch's location on cleared land once part of an old orchard of the Hall estate.

A contest was held in 1926 to select a new mascot, with the $25 prize going to the author of the winning entry—Golden Flashes. Oliver Wolcott, one of Kent's first football stars, perpetuated this name as sports editor of the local newspaper. Mascots and symbols have ranged from lightning bolt logos to a golden retriever named Mac the Flash to the current golden eagle mascot, Flash.

Music department head Anne Maud Shamel established the Kent State marching band in 1919, and it began playing at football games as a field band as early as 1920. Pictured here are members of the 1928 band. The following year, Roy D. Metcalf assumed directorship in a career that would last until his death in 1957.

Women in the Midwest, including at Kent State, began to make cheerleading a coed activity by the 1920s. As a teacher training college, women comprised the majority of the school's student population in the early years, and this was reflected in every area of student life, including athletics and cheerleading. The 1928 pep squad is shown here.

Dr. Arville O. DeWeese served at Kent State for 41 years (1924–1965). He was appointed as the head of the Departments of Health Service and Health and Physical Education and remained director of both departments for 22 years. DeWeese helped organize the American School Health Association and served as president and national officer in that organization for many years. When Pres. John Edward McGilvrey created the new Department of Physical and Health Education that also had oversight for athletic coaching, he recruited DeWeese to serve as its first director. The university honored his service to KSU with a new health center dedicated in his name in 1969.

George J. Altmann (left) came to Kent in 1927 as a professor of health and physical education. He helped create the Phi Epsilon Kappa physical education fraternity. He actively engaged in the intramural program for many years and coached the men's "gym team" (gymnastics), pictured below, starting in 1931. He also served as a judge for the annual American Turner's gymnastics competition for over 25 years. During World War II, Altmann was the head of the university's portion of physical education for the Army Air Corps stationed on campus. He retired from KSU in 1958, completing 31 years of service, and a residence hall was dedicated in his honor in 1969.

Following a hiatus in campus construction due to the war, Wills Gymnasium was built in 1923 for $175,000, becoming the hub of physical education, intramural, recreational, and varsity sport and including a swimming pool in the basement. It was formally dedicated in 1925 along with the establishment of a four-year course in physical and health education and athletic coaching.

In 1927, athletic director Merle E. Wagoner, along with student-athletes Eugene J. Feeley, August Peterka, and others, came up with the idea of forming a Varsity K Club—a social organization for varsity lettermen. Early activities included organizing dances, the first fall homecoming event, and running an annual High School Day (to entice high school athletes to attend Kent State). The members shown here are posed in K formation.

The diversity of individual and team sports present throughout the long history of women's intramural activity is striking. In the first half of the 20th century, in addition to the longtime standby sports of basketball, tennis, and baseball, women engaged in sports such as indoor baseball, horseshoes, swimming, synchronized swimming, table tennis, badminton, archery, bowling, handball, field hockey (below), and soccer. Lucille Hendricks, pictured at left, won the 1928–1929 horseshoe championship. Male students also participated in intramural sports. The 1924 *Chestnut Burr* reported the following: "Believing that athletics for the many is far superior to athletics for the few, Kent State, during the past year, has carried out an extensive intramural program." Supervised by Frank N. Harsh, new director of men's physical education, the year's intramural schedule included competition in speedball, cross-country, volleyball, foul shooting, and horseshoe pitching.

Multisport athlete Eugene J. Feeley '27 played football, basketball, and baseball. He served as captain of the basketball and football teams and also as president of the fledgling Varsity K Club. In recognition of his play at Kent, Feeley was inducted into the Varsity K Hall of Fame (the Kent State athletics hall of fame) with the second class of honorees in 1980.

Leslie P. Hardy '28, another multisport athlete and early hall of fame inductee, lettered in track and basketball. Like many early students, Hardy was fully engaged in campus life, within the relatively small student body of that time. He worked on the staff of the *Kentonian*, *Kent Stater*, and yearbook publications. He served on student council and was a social science club member and a fraternity member.

Merle E. Wagoner (second from left) was named football coach in 1925. He also coached basketball and baseball. Although his overall records were not highly successful, he brought intercollegiate standards into practice at Kent and ushered the school's acceptance into the Ohio Athletic Conference. His coaching career at Kent ended in 1933 as a result of a push for a change in coaching staff initiated by the trustees.

While early physical education curriculums were largely comprised of gymnastics, or systems of movement, as shown here, by the 1920s the emphasis was shifting to play, games, and sport as the basis for physical education. The gymnastics movement reflected utilitarian beliefs and justifications for the importance of physical education, making it more acceptable as a component of education.

3

ESTABLISHMENT OF
VARSITY ATHLETICS
1930–1939

The 1930s marked a shift toward an emphasis on varsity athletics and less concern with their direct connection to the education curriculum. Kent State had already expanded from a normal school to a college, offering traditional liberal studies degree programs, and in 1935, the institution was granted university status by the State of Ohio. The board of trustees and alumni felt that a strong intercollegiate athletic program (for men), particularly emphasizing football, was key to further distinguishing KSU within the region and in the state. Perhaps one of the most significant appointments made during this period was that of Joseph Begala, initially hired as a football coach, who went on to coach nearly every sport offered at Kent and eventually became a legendary figure in KSU wrestling history. Begala also coached Kent's first Ohio Athletic Conference championship team—the 1934 golf team. In 1935, George Donald Starn was appointed as head football coach and director of varsity athletics, with Begala relegated to assistant football coach.

As intercollegiate competition became institutionalized, a number of individual athletes began to distinguish themselves in wrestling, track, football, and baseball, and the wrestling teams of this period boasted several Olympic finalists.

For female students, athletics remained closely tied to both curricular and extracurricular activities through participation in physical education courses and intramurals. As in the preceding decades, women competed in a remarkable variety of individual and team sports. Intramural action was enthusiastically reported in campus publications, and the motto of the Women's Athletic Association (WAA) at this time, Play for Play's Sake, captured the intended, somewhat limited focus of athletics for women. This matched the national women's physical education movement, which continued the philosophy of "a girl for every sport, a sport for every girl" and downplayed elite athletics.

Although Wills Gymnasium had been dedicated in 1924, the need for new and expanded facilities was already being felt in the 1930s. Expansion of facilities, including a stadium, were planned but were not funded due to the financial strains of the Great Depression.

Coach Joseph Begala (back, far left) came to Kent in 1929, leading the KSU grapplers, one of his most successful endeavors, to a 282-68-5 record during his 39-year tenure. His success started early with his first two undefeated seasons in 1935 and 1936. His 1933 grapplers pictured here also won the Ohio intercollegiate championship.

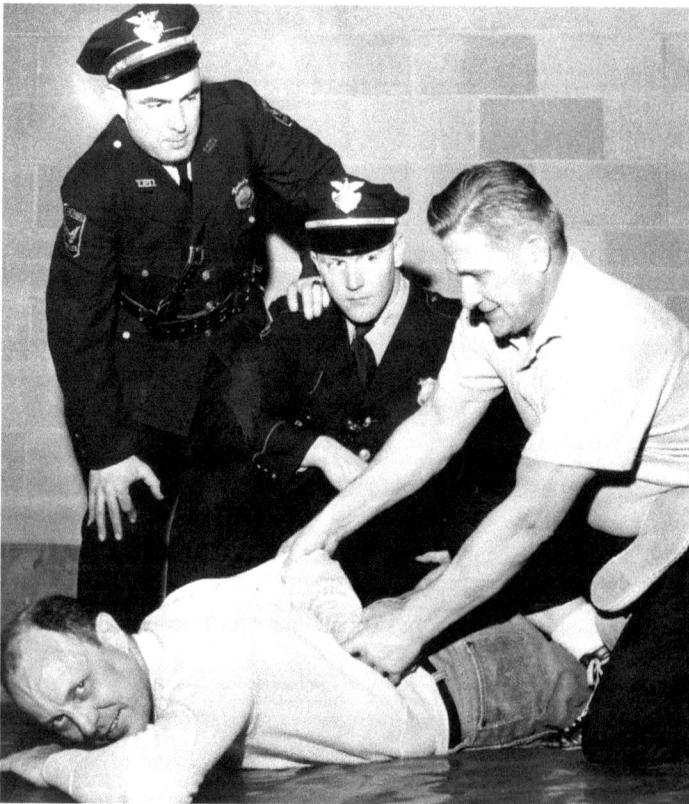

Kent's "Iron Man" not only distinguished himself in coaching, during World War II Joseph Begala served in the U.S. Navy, discharged in 1946 at the lieutenant commander rank. An expert in hand-to-hand combat and self-defense, Begala coauthored the 1943 edition of the U.S. Navy and Marine Corps *Hand-to-Hand Combat* manual. Begala's teaching career extended beyond campus as he regularly provided self-defense training to the law enforcement community.

One of Begala's early standout wrestlers, Art Stejskal '31 contributed to Kent's early success in wrestling. He won the Ohio state championship at 175 pounds in 1930 and at heavyweight in 1931. He served as captain of the squad in 1931 and made it to the Amateur Athletic Union (AAU) finals in 1932.

Art Stejskal
Ohio State Champion
175# 1930
Heavy 1931
Captain 1931
A.A.U. finals 1932 New York City

Buell "Bud" Graven '38 wrestled his way to three seasons undefeated in dual-meet competition and won the Lake Erie AAU championship four times. Varsity captain in 1938, Graven recorded some of the fastest pins of his era, including seven seconds in the 1936 Berlin Olympic semifinals. He posted a 59-1-1 collegiate record as a Flash.

Another of Kent's star wrestlers, Carmen Falcone '41 also excelled on the gridiron, scoring five touchdowns in one game against the State University of New York at Buffalo in 1938. Falcone became the first All-America grappler for KSU with his third-place finish in the heavyweight division at the NCAA championship meet in 1939.

The 1934 golf team earned KSU's first Ohio Athletic Conference title. Coached by Joseph Begala (center), the team finished with an undefeated, untied record (6-0). They faced only three other schools that season—Wooster, Mount Union, and Akron—playing each twice. The championship status was decided on the best season record as no tournaments would be held until after World War II.

George Donald Starn (below, back left) was appointed as head football coach and director of varsity athletics in 1935 as part of KSU's initiative to improve its athletic programs and the football program, in particular. Students and alumni opposed Starn's appointment and pressured university administration to appoint a more prominent coach. In addition, Joseph Begala had been serving as head football coach since 1933, along with successfully coaching wrestling and other sports. Starn's appointment was upheld, however, and during his eight years at Kent, he went on to establish a 34-28-2 record. He resigned after enlisting in the navy during World War II.

While softball took hold in church and industrial leagues around the country, many women, such as these intramural ball players at KSU (1932), played baseball on college campuses. Like many midwestern universities, KSU was racially integrated, if only inconsistently, well before the civil rights movement made that the norm throughout the United States.

This action photograph of a baseball game or practice shows evidence of the "rustic" circumstances under which outdoor sports were played at that time. This photograph likely dates from the mid-1930s. Campus maps of that period show the athletic field located directly behind the power plant (center). The proposed site of new athletic fields was along East Summit Street, southeast of the location shown here.

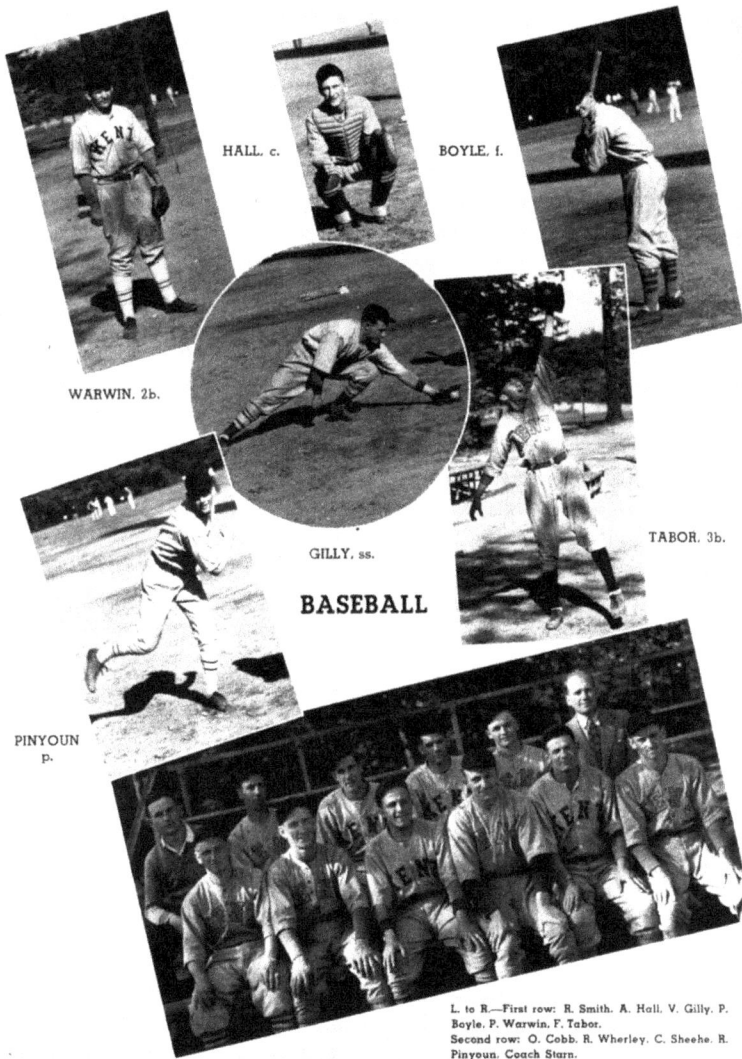

HALL. c.

BOYLE. f.

WARWIN. 2b.

GILLY. ss.

TABOR. 3b.

BASEBALL

PINYOUN
p.

L. to R.—First row: R. Smith. A. Hall. V. Gilly. P.
Boyle. P. Warwin. F. Tabor.
Second row: O. Cobb. R. Wherley. C. Sheehe. R.
Pinyoun. Coach Starn.

In the late 1930s, KSU baseball began boasting some outstanding individual players. In the succeeding decades, the program would go on to produce a number of prominent players, many of whom went on to professional careers. This photographic montage from the 1937 yearbook includes standout pitcher Randy "Roy" Pinyoun '38 (left center image), who lettered three times in baseball and basketball. After graduating, he signed a professional contract with the Cleveland Indians and would go on to play for five seasons in the Carolina League. After Pinyoun's departure, another star emerged—Michael Feduniak '42—who earned nine varsity Ks as a multisport athlete in baseball, basketball, and football. He played professionally for the Boston Red Sox and was invited to tryouts for both the Pittsburgh Steelers and Detroit Lions football teams, opting for baseball instead. Feduniak was also distinguished by his military career. He served as a flight leader for the 315th Troop Carrier Squadron of the 10th Air Force and was awarded the Distinguished Flying Cross on two occasions, the Air Medal three times, and several other decorations.

In the early 20th century, physical education transitioned from gymnastics (systems of calisthenics or human movement) to sport and dance. Natural dance, as demonstrated here, became a central component of the women's physical education movement, while men's physical education became more aligned with sport. Eventually both dance and athletics separated from their physical education roots, as happened at KSU in 1971 (athletics) and 1995 (dance).

The WAA offered a wide range of sports and activities. In the 1936–1937 school year, for example, the WAA included team activities such as Shark's Club (synchronized swimming), hiking, basketball, deck tennis, badminton, baseball, and tap dancing. Individual activities ranged from bowling and horseshoes to archery (shown here), darts, and golf.

Considered one of the all-time great early KSU athletes, Charles "Cocky" Kilbourne '32 earned 11 letters in football, basketball, baseball, track, and tennis. He set a school record in 1929 for the longest punt (99 yards) and was named an All-Ohio fullback. Football coach Merle E. Wagoner deemed Kilbourne one of the greatest players he had ever seen.

Another prominent early KSU athlete was Theodore (Ted) Sapp '31, who lettered in football, basketball, baseball, and wrestling. He was one of the small group of students who cofounded the Varsity K organization. A native of Kent, he remained in the area after college and maintained a lifelong interest in KSU athletics. He founded the athletics booster club known now as the Blue and Gold Club.

Marvin "Lefty" Garner '39 made his mark in KSU baseball history by pitching the school's first no-hitter in 1936 against Ashland College. Garner, who also lettered in football, basketball, and track, went on to play professional baseball for the Detroit Tigers' Triple-A club, but his career was cut short by an arm injury. He practiced dentistry in Canton for 36 years, following military service in World War II.

All-around athlete Leslie "Swede" Netzen played football for KSU from 1937 to 1939, serving as captain in 1939 under coach George Donald Starn. He particularly starred in track and field as a multievent competitor, averaging 25 points per meet on his own. He placed sixth in the U.S. national championships in the decathlon in 1940.

4

WAR READINESS AND
PHYSICAL EDUCATION

1940–1949

Just as KSU was beginning to chart success in its intercollegiate athletics programs (the football team's record was improving steadily, wrestling had won nine interstate tournaments in 10 years, and baseball boasted its first player to go on to the majors), World War II brought normal life to a halt. After the United States' entry into the war, campus enrollment plummeted, and the student body, once again, consisted almost entirely of female students. In March 1943, the 336th College Training Detachment of the Army Air Corps was stationed at the university, resulting in a suspension of many ordinary campus activities, including intercollegiate athletics. Almost all sports activities during the war years revolved around two things: traditional recreational play and athletic fitness as related to war readiness. The WAA's agenda included the typical array of sports competitions and related events but also involved activities tied to the war such as increased physical fitness training, military drills, strength training, obstacle course programs, hikes, and health drives. This new focus was articulated in the 1942 yearbook's report on WAA activities: "The Women's Athletic Association has emphasized this year the importance of good health of students for national defense and the war effort."

While maintaining its regular curriculum, the university, under the leadership of its war activity council, implemented a number of changes. It instituted a quarter system that allowed for quicker completion of degrees. Special premilitary and war industry courses were added to the curriculum. These included a slate of health and physical education "premilitary training" courses for men and women going into the armed services, such as a special water-safety class that covered endurance swimming, swimming underwater beneath simulated burning oil, and other training related to combat situations.

Even as the university put building projects on hold during the war, planning continued for anticipated expanded housing, educational, and athletic needs after the war. The second half of the decade marked a return to university expansion with enrollments moving toward all-time highs. Intercollegiate sports programs were reenergized, raising expectations for a new era in athletics.

A photographic collage from the 1941 yearbook shows women engaged in WAA activities. The organization would shift focus in the following year, taking on several war-related activities. Despite the changes brought about by America's entry into the world war, the largely female student population on campus would continue many of the traditional athletic competitions and social activities coordinated by the WAA since 1914.

Physical education classes provided arenas for coeducational sports interactions. Pictured here are the physical education classes of professors Virginia Harvey and George J. Altmann in a volleyball match. The 1940 yearbook indicated that "co-educational gym classes are a regular part of the university curriculum, another field in which KSU has pioneered."

Although Wills Gymnasium had been hailed as one of Ohio's finest athletic facilities at the time of its formal dedication in 1925, KSU entered the 1940s finding itself once again in need of improved and expanded indoor and outdoor athletics facilities. Financial shortfalls during the Great Depression stalled most building plans of the 1930s, but modest improvements, such as the construction of new tennis courts behind Wills Gymnasium (above) and clearing of the former college farm for the installation of athletic fields (below) were made near the start of the 1940s. The war would postpone the realization of more extensive improvements until the beginning of the following decade.

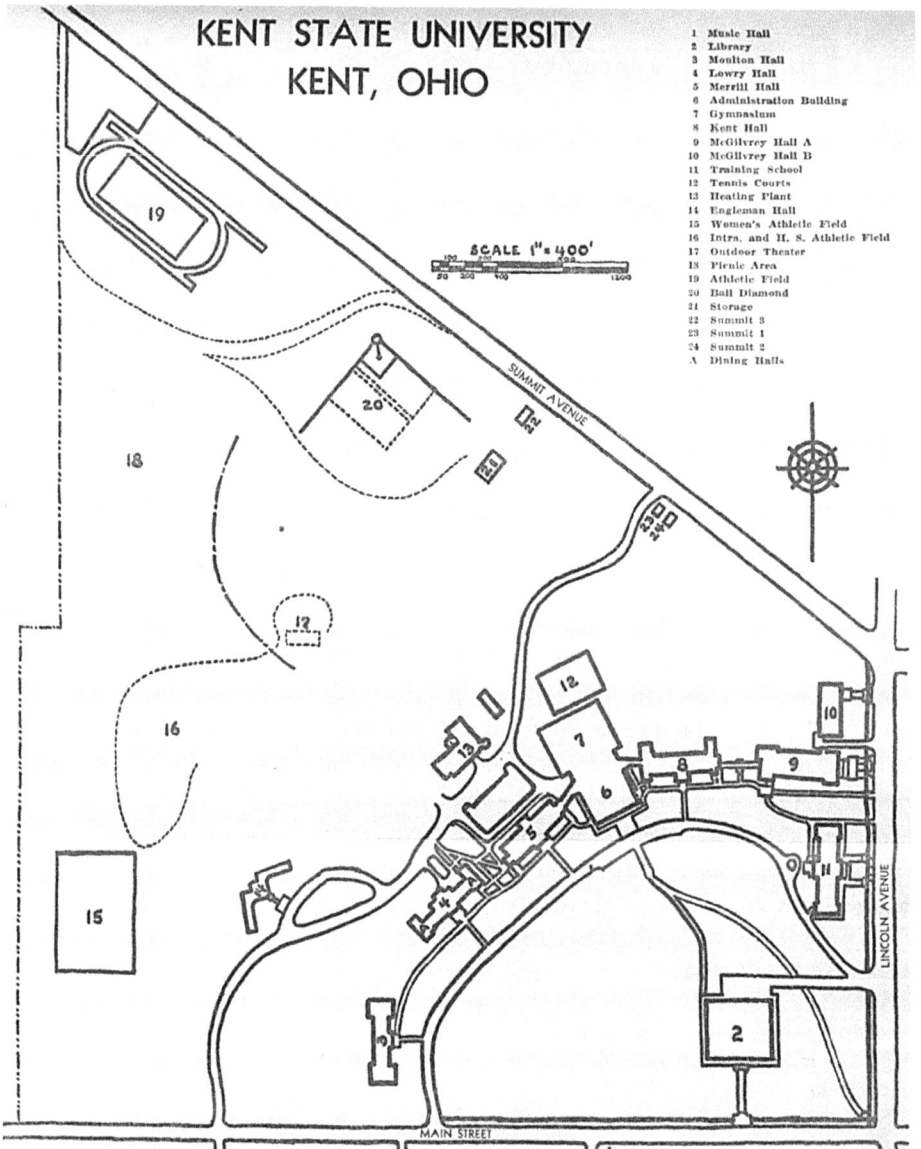

KENT STATE UNIVERSITY
KENT, OHIO

SCALE 1"=400'

1 Music Hall
2 Library
3 Moulton Hall
4 Lowry Hall
5 Merrill Hall
6 Administration Building
7 Gymnasium
8 Kent Hall
9 McGilvrey Hall A
10 McGilvrey Hall B
11 Training School
12 Tennis Courts
13 Heating Plant
14 Engleman Hall
15 Women's Athletic Field
16 Intra. and H. S. Athletic Field
17 Outdoor Theater
18 Picnic Area
19 Athletic Field
20 Ball Diamond
21 Storage
22 Summit 3
23 Summit 1
24 Summit 2
A Dining Halls

This 1941 campus map shows the location of various athletic facilities at that time. Wills Gymnasium is located at the rear of the administration building at No. 7 with the tennis courts directly behind the gymnasium, designated as No. 12. The baseball diamond and men's athletic field and track are pictured at 20 and 19, respectively. Women's, intramural, and high school sports facilities are located behind the heating plant and Engleman Hall in the areas numbered 15 and 16. At this time, the Kent campus was comprised of a roughly triangular footprint within the boundaries of Main Street (State Route 59), Lincoln Street, and Summit Street in what is today referred to as Front Campus. Improvement and expansion of athletic facilities would be put on hold during the war years. New building projects would commence in the coming decade as the campus started expanding its boundaries to areas along East Main Street and farther southeast along Summit Street.

Unseeded Michael Slepecky '50 earned All-America honors in the 1941 NCAA championship meet at 128 pounds. As the yearbook describes it, "Little Mike Slepecky, a veritable whirlwind, whipped a former champ and placed second to give KSU a fifth place among the nation's top ranking grapplers." Slepecky's career, like that of many, would be interrupted by the war, but he returned in 1948 to resume his educational and wrestling endeavors.

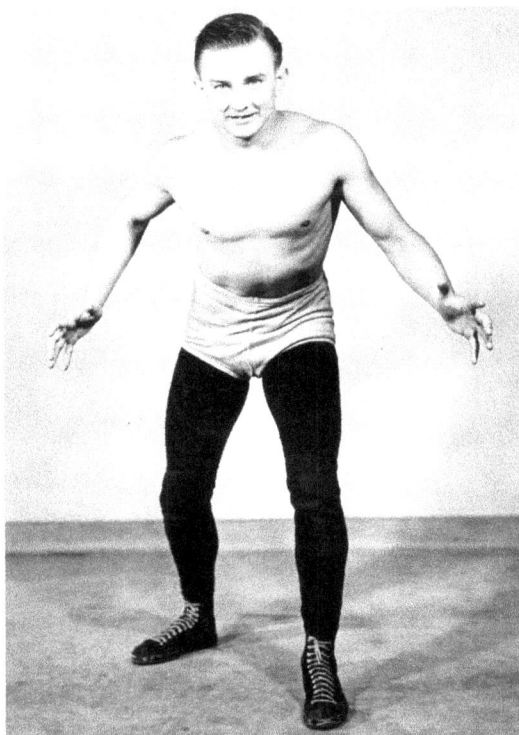

Walter Porowski matched Slepecky for the highest placing by a KSU wrestler with his second at the NCAA championships in 1942 in the heavyweight division, earning All-America honors, which helped the team to its highest finish, a tie for fifth. His teammate Robert Bader also achieved All-America status with his fourth-place finish at 165 pounds.

Although racially integrated since its founding, there is scant evidence before the 1940s of fuller racial integration within varsity athletics at KSU. The 1940s, especially the postwar years, would see an increased level of racial diversity among athletes, particularly in track and field, as shown here, which had always offered integrated competition at the national level in the United States. Like other northern and midwestern universities, KSU offered limited opportunities for black students and athletes. Yet, like the military, which faced pressure and eventually an executive order (9981) to end racial segregation and discrimination, civil rights considerations began in earnest in universities at the end of the 1940s. Despite partial racial integration, including segregated student housing and housing segregation in the city of Kent, there is evidence that KSU refused to play football against segregated southern teams if it meant leaving black players off the field.

KSU TO RECEIVE 500 CADETS

KENT STATER

Kent State University Student Newspaper

Vol. XVIII Z-568   KENT, OHIO, FRIDAY, MARCH 12, 1943   No. 66

Army Air Force Officals Send Approval Last Night

A telegram from army air force officials at Maxwell field, Ala., last night indicated that Kent has been approved for a quota of 500 aviation cadets, Dr. K. C. Leebrick, University

The *Kent Stater* headline (above) announces the planned arrival of the 336th College Training Detachment of the Army Air Corps in the spring of 1943. The group's presence on campus brought many changes to campus life. Varsity athletics were suspended indefinitely. Student dormitories were filled to capacity by military trainees, forcing the mostly female student body of 450 to secure off-campus housing. In addition to accommodating the Army Air Corps, the university developed a number of special programs, functioning as a civilian agency supporting the nation's military efforts. It provided the equivalent to today's distance education programs, offering correspondence courses for those enlisted in the military, and also operated six military reserve programs and a Civil Aeronautics Authority war training service.

MILITARY AREA
RESTRICTED
336TH C.T.D.(A.C.)
U.S.ARMY AIRFORCES
CLOSED 6P.M.-6A.M.
BY ORDER OF C.O.

The suspension of varsity athletics finally ended with the assemblage of a basketball team during the 1944–1945 season. Football soon followed. The 1946 football team came to stand for a new era in KSU sports and was remarkable in several ways. It was comprised almost entirely of freshmen, most of them returning war veterans. Despite many of the players' inexperience at the collegiate level and a lack of adequate equipment and practice facilities, the team managed a 6-2 record for the season. Coaching staff was comprised of new head football coach and director of athletics Trevor J. Rees, assisted by Harry Adams, Karl G. Chesnutt, Wes Stevens, and Joseph Begala. Standout players included Wilbur "Wib" Little, George Kovalik, Frank Mesek, and John Moore. Among this history-making team's players were future KSU coaches Richard Paskert and Richard Kotis.

1946 KENT STATE FOOTBALL TEAM

30 year reunion   **oct. 29, 1976**

RUSTY NAIL RESTAURANT

1946 FOOTBALL TEAM

	WON 6		LOST 2
KSU	40	HIRAM	0
KSU	20	JOHN CARROLL	7
KSU	39	BLUFFTON	0
KSU	17	KALAMAZOO	0
KSU	0	(HC) BOWLING GREEN	13
KSU	12	BALDWIN WALLACE	21
KSU	7	OHIO WESLEYAN	0
KSU	13	AKRON UNIVERSITY	6

A POSSIBLE STARTING ELEVEN
LINE— SUA, PASKERT, KUHNER, McGROARTY, MARO, SHEINBART, TOTH.
BACKS— GERBITZ, MARKOVITCH, NELSON, WOLFGRAM.

WES STEVENS & JOE BEGALA PLUS THE KENT STATE GOLDEN FLASHES
BENCH PULL TOGETHER FOR A SCORE.

TREVOR J. "TREV" REES
HEAD COACH

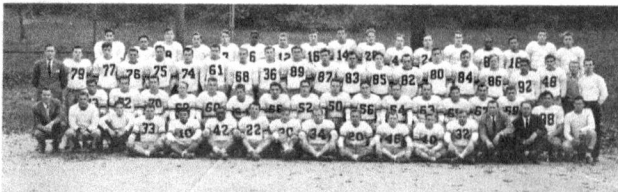

COACHING STAFF
TREV REES, COACH

HARRY ADAMS, KARL CHESNUTT,
WES STEVENS - ASST. COACHES

JOE BEGALA, TRAINER
RALPH GARMUS, HONORARY CAPTAIN ELECT

WILBUR "WIB" LITTLE
HALFBACK
ALL OHIO CONFERENCE - 1944, 1945

WELCOME TO ALL

THE LONG KALAMAZOO TRIP BY TRAIN

THE LONG KALAMAZOO TRIP BY TRAIN

Running back Wib Little led the football team in rushing and scoring for two of his three years on the squad. His career total of 2,109 yards, with an average of 7 yards per carry, helped him to earn All–Ohio Athletic Conference honors. Little was another early inductee into the Varsity K Hall of Fame.

As a member of the Golden Flash football team, James (Jimmy) Jones '46 lettered three years, was named second-team Little All-American in 1939, and received All-Ohio and all-conference recognition in 1940. Jones signed a professional contract and had a tryout with the Detroit Lions in 1941. He played semiprofessional ball with the El Toro (California) Marines in 1944 and the Cherry Point Marines in 1945.

World War II veteran and wrestling captain Gene Glass earned All-America status in 1946 with a fourth-place finish at the NCAA championship meet. The same year, he finished third in the AAU national meet. Glass continued his military service in the Korean War and was later killed in a military training accident in 1954 in Jacksonville, Florida.

One of KSU's most accomplished Olympic athletes, weight lifter Peter T. George '52, a three-time Olympian, won two silver medals (1948 and 1956) and a gold medal at the Helsinki Games in 1952 in the middleweight division. He also captured Pan American gold in 1953. He served as team captain and coach of the KSU weight lifting club.

Multisport athlete Joseph Kotys '56 earned letters in gymnastics, swimming, and wrestling at KSU. He won the AAU gymnastics titles on long horse (vault) and parallel bars. He garnered NCAA gymnastics all-around titles in 1949–1950 and individual NCAA titles on parallel bars in 1949 and 1950, the horizontal bar in 1950, and pommel horse in 1951. He was a U.S. Olympic team member in 1948 and 1956.

A four-year letterman in basketball, George Fulton '51 was selected for the All–Ohio Athletic Conference team in 1949–1950 and 1950–1951 and earned honorable mention All-America status during his senior year. The men's basketball program, under coaches Harry Adams and David McDowell, enjoyed a highly successful period in the late 1940s and early 1950s. During Fulton's career, the teams earned a four-season record of 71-28, for a .720 winning percentage.

KSU is today an eight-campus university, with regional campuses having been established throughout the northeast Ohio region. One of the largest and oldest of these is the Stark campus (originally established as the Canton campus in 1946). Students at regional campuses have also taken part in the athletic and intramural life of the university. These images from the 1948 and 1949 Canton campus annual highlight some of the years' sports activities. Basketball appeared to be the sport of predominant interest, but the campus also had golf, baseball, and tennis teams, all of which faced off against high school and college teams at this time. Shown here are members of the campus WAA and the men's intramural basketball team. From at least the 1960s on, there have been intracampus competitions among regional campus teams.

5

THE MID-AMERICAN CONFERENCE

1950–1959

In 1950, the university's long years of planning for new athletic facilities finally came to fruition with the dedication of the men's physical education building and Memorial Stadium. Both facilities were dedicated in honor of KSU's war dead. Pres. George Bowman's address at the stadium dedication ceremony expressed the fulfillment of the school's long-held dreams for improved facilities. "This structure has been in the hopes and aspirations of the students and faculty and friends of the University since the first athletic competition more than three decades ago. . . . While this structure is only the start of what we all hope will be ultimately completed here, we no longer will feel apologetic for our facilities for outdoor athletic contests." The new facilities were the center of men's intercollegiate athletic and physical education programs, while Wills Gymnasium remained the site of women's physical education and intramural programs.

In 1951, KSU was admitted into the Mid-American Conference (MAC). While wrestling and baseball had maintained consistently solid programs throughout the 1930s and 1940s, the football program charted some significant improvements in the 1950s, under coach Trevor J. Rees, making an appearance in the 1954 Refrigerator Bowl. Out of only 25 winning seasons in 86 years of KSU football, nine came in the 1950s.

The 1950s signaled a return to the wide range of athletic and social activities organized by the WAA, with the addition of less athletic and more socially oriented activities such as bridge and square dancing. A shift in the name of the organization echoed this new focus as the local chapter evolved into the Women's Recreation Association (WRA) during this period. However, it was also during this decade when gymnast Betty Jean Maycock became one of KSU's first female athletes to attain national and international standing as a member of the 1959 Pan American team and a 1960 U.S. Olympic team member. Maycock's accomplishments, along with the arrival of dynamic coaching team Janet and Rudy Bachna in 1959, marked the beginning of a distinguished KSU gymnastics program that would continue for many years.

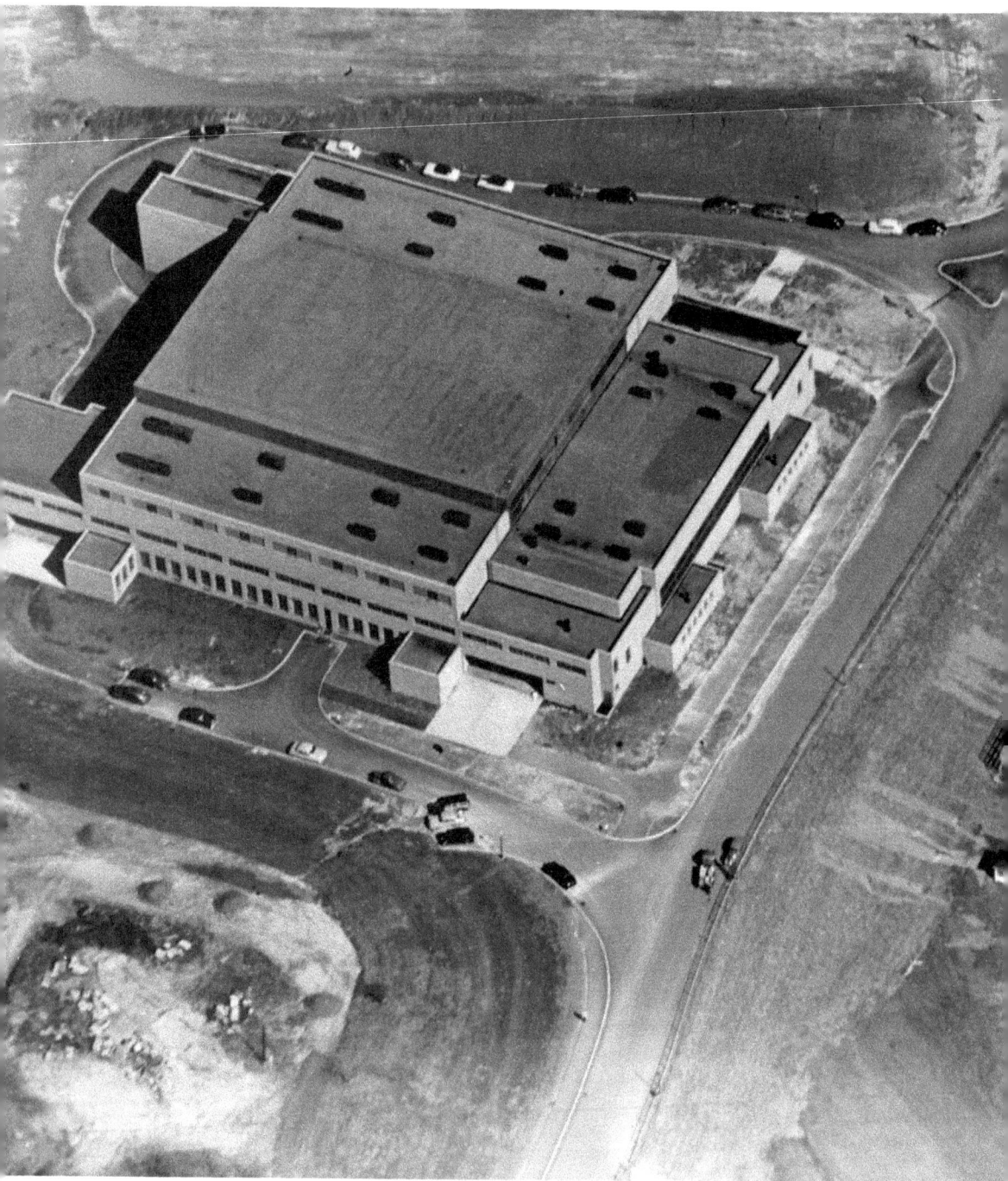

The year 1950 was marked as a historic year in KSU athletics as two major facilities were constructed—a stadium and men's gymnasium shown here in aerial view. The men's physical education building (later renamed Memorial Gymnasium) was built for $1.3 million and was considered "one of the finest in the entire Midwest." This 110,000-square-foot facility had a seating capacity of 10,000 and included an Olympic-size pool, handball courts, and modern

locker rooms, as well as classrooms and administrative offices and spacious ticketing and lobby areas. Named in memory of the 113 KSU students and alumni who died in World War II, Memorial Stadium was dedicated in 1950 and had a seating capacity of 5,600. The stadium was located in front of the new gymnasium, adjacent to Summit Street where today a large visitors' parking lot is located.

Jack "Wahoo" Mancos '53, who played football and baseball, was one of the most versatile backs in KSU history. In his most impressive game, he scored five touchdowns against Western Michigan, including three on pass receptions. Here Mancos (No. 46) is flanked by first-team All-MAC picks Joe Barbee (No. 87) and Jim Cullom (No. 33). These early football stars led the team to a third-place finish in their first season in the MAC.

Political science and pre-law graduate Penfield Tate '53, KSU's first gridiron All-American with his selection by the International News Service to the first team in 1952, was a three-time letter winner (1950–1952). Tate earned his law degree in 1968 at the University of Colorado and later became mayor of Boulder.

Grappler Jack Love, two-time MAC
champion at 123 pounds (1954 and
1955), earned All-America honors
with a fourth-place finish at the
NCAA championships at 115 pounds
in 1954. He earned his bachelor's
degree in industrial arts in 1955 and
went on to win the AAU national
tournament at 115 pounds in 1956.

Two-sport athlete Daniel Potopsky '56
played baseball and basketball for KSU in
the mid-1950s. The top-scoring basketball
player averaged 23.4 points per game for
the 1954–1955 season and ended with
1,122 points for his career. He led the KSU
nine in hitting three of his four years,
earned All-MAC honors in 1956, and
ended with a fielding percentage of .968 for
his baseball career.

The football team saw its first postseason play in the 1954 Evansville, Indiana, Jaycees/Junior Chamber of Commerce Refrigerator Bowl against the University of Delaware Blue Hens. KSU lost 19-7, but for many, the excitement of seeing KSU in a bowl game far outweighed the disappointment of the loss. Prior to the game, the athletic department received a telegram from an alumnus (the 1925 team's quarterback) desperately seeking tickets and noting a willingness to travel 300 miles to see the game, who quipped, "I have waited a long time to see Kent State in a big time bowl game." This success came right in the middle of coach Trevor J. Rees's 18 years at the helm as the Flashes' longest-serving football coach. (Courtesy of the Evansville Jaycees/Junior Chamber of Commerce.)

Lou Holtz '59 earned a Varsity K as a linebacker on the Golden Flash grid squad in 1957. He went on to become one of the most successful college football coaches in the country in a career that included positions at the University of Iowa, the University of South Carolina, the Ohio State University, the University of Arkansas, the University of Minnesota, and the University of Notre Dame. In 20 seasons as a head coach, Holtz compiled a 153-76-5 record.

Luke Owens played as an offensive end and defensive tackle at KSU, where he also lettered twice in track as a shot-putter and discus thrower. He was selected as an All-American by two rating services in 1956. Owens was drafted into the NFL in 1957 by the Baltimore Colts and then played for several years for the Chicago and St. Louis Cardinals (1958–1965).

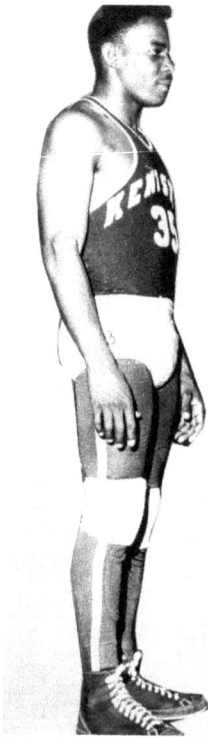

Continuing the tradition of grappling success, wrestler Clarence McNair '59, captain of the team, gained All-America prestige with his fourth place at 130 pounds at the NCAA championships in 1959. He won at the MAC championships twice (1957 and 1958) and ended his career with a 47-7-1 record for a .861 winning percentage.

Grappler Pat Semary posted a 59-8 record wrestling for KSU from 1957 to 1960. He went undefeated his sophomore and senior seasons, winning the MAC championships in 1960 at 134 pounds. Semary earned All-America status with a fourth-place finish at the 1960 NCAA championships at 137 pounds. He graduated with a degree in art in 1961.

Coach Matt Resick (right) led the KSU baseball team from 1949 to 1961, posting a 132-100-1 record, with winning seasons 10 of his 13 years. He coached 10 future professional players. Along with his coaching duties, Resick served as a professor and administrator in the School of Health, Physical Education, and Recreation (1948–1975).

Dale Reichert '63 (left) lettered in baseball and basketball at KSU in the late 1950s, leaving school in 1959 after being signed by the Los Angeles Dodgers to their Kokomo, Indiana, minor-league team. He was named the league's Rookie of the Year in 1959. After additional years playing in the minors, he returned to KSU in the early 1960s to complete his education.

One of many future professional baseball players to come from KSU, Richard (Rich) Rollins '60, a .389 career hitter for the Flashes, earned All-MAC second baseman three times (1958–1960). He signed with the major-league Washington Senators and moved with the team to Minnesota. The American League honored him as Rookie of the Year (1962). He later played professionally in Seattle and Cleveland.

This 1957 photograph shows an indoor batting cage that was created from a converted storage room in Memorial Gymnasium, allowing baseball players to practice indoors during the early spring months when lingering wintry weather in northeast Ohio made outdoor practice nearly impossible. The 1957 season was hindered by extremely poor weather, and the team's first three games were cancelled due to snow, sleet, and rain.

Eugene "Stick" Michael '67 excelled at baseball and basketball for KSU in 1958. He rejected a chance to play professional basketball, opting for a career in baseball instead, signing with the Pittsburgh Pirates in 1959. He closed out his major-league playing career in 1976 after playing for the Dodgers, Yankees, Tigers, and Red Sox. He then served as manager and executive for several professional teams.

Gymnast Betty Jean (Maycock) Harrington '64 attended Kent State University High School in the late 1950s. She won the 1958 Junior National Amateur Athletic Union all-around trophy and the 1959 AAU floor exercise title. Maycock represented the United States at the 1959 Pan American championships and the 1960 Tokyo Olympic Games.

Homecoming as a fall weekend event paired with a football game was not instituted at KSU until the 1920s. In the post–World War II years, this annual weekend fete would reach a pinnacle of popularity, becoming a highlight of the academic year, complete with parade, homecoming queen, and special football game halftime events. The photograph above shows the 1954 queen, Marilyn Kapcar, being honored at halftime, surrounded by members of KSU's Twin Bands in heart-shaped formation. Band director Roy Metcalf was perhaps best known for his introduction in 1940 of the KSU Twin Bands—matching all-female and all-male bands that performed in tandem, to much acclaim. The photograph at left shows 1958 queen Judy Barchfeld's coronation, complete with a special ROTC Scabbard and Blade group display.

6

INDIVIDUAL SUCCESS

1960–1969

As the university marked its semicentennial, it was continuing on a path of further expansion both of its academic programs and physical facilities. During the decade, KSU launched its first doctoral degree programs, constructed several new buildings on the Kent campus, and established additional regional campus centers within northeast Ohio. While few athletic programs would enjoy consistent success throughout the 1960s, a number of excellent athletes arose, particularly in baseball, track, cross-country, and gymnastics.

Compared with previous decades, women's intramural activities received only limited reporting in the yearbooks of the late 1950s and early 1960s. Although there is evidence that women's intramural teams organized some limited competition with nearby schools for many years, the mid-1960s marked the first time that women's teams and their intercollegiate records were reported in the annual. Under coach Fay Biles, the 1963 field hockey team boasted the only winning record of any varsity team (male or female) that year, finishing with an undefeated record for the season. Meanwhile, women's gymnastics under Janet Bachna continued to thrive. During this time, the Lady Flashes participated in the national championships organized by precursors to the Association for Intercollegiate Athletics for Women (AIAW) for 11 consecutive years, and gymnast Marie (Walther) Bilski competed at the international level in the Olympics and other venues.

In men's competition, baseball, basketball, and football struggled with lukewarm records while track and field developed greater strength during the decade, particularly in distance running led by KSU's first sub-four-minute miler, Sam Bair, cross-country great Pete Lorandeau, and three-miler Art Coolidge III. Baseball sensation catcher Thurman Munson made his mark on KSU record books in the late 1960s as he paired with another baseball great, pitcher Steve Stone.

The 1960s marked a time of growing challenges for collegiate athletics from escalating costs and from the civil rights movement, solidified in the 1964 Civil Rights Act and supported by student activism. These challenges would lead to significant changes in the 1970s with a restructuring of the NCAA and greater educational rights for minorities and women.

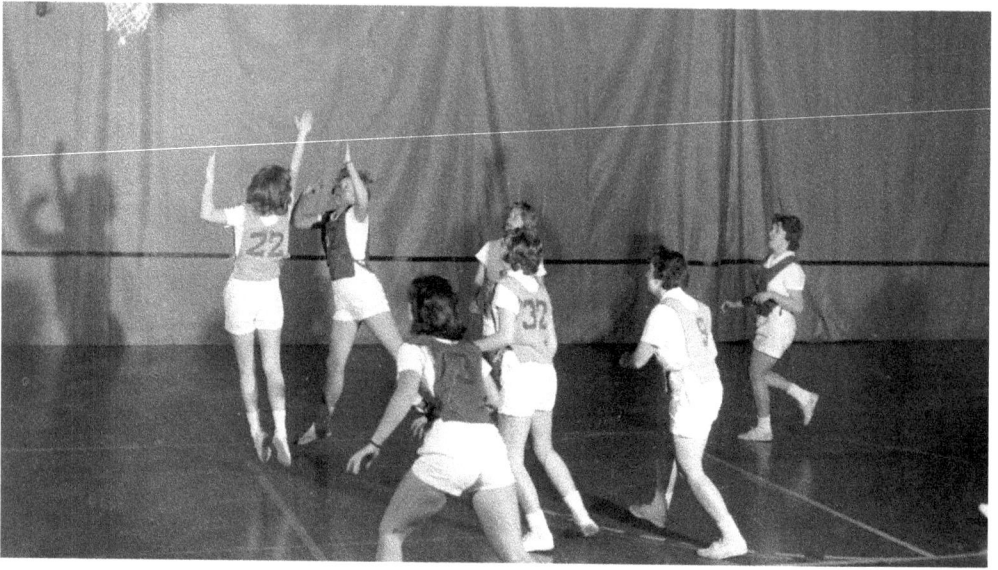

Directed by Dr. Beverly Seidel and Dr. Carl Erickson, the Division of Health, Physical Education, and Athletics offered students a bachelor of science degree in education as well as master of science and master of education degrees. Both of the images shown here were used in the division's marketing publications of the early 1960s. With separate programs for women and men, the women's program tried to promote a positive, and traditionally gender appropriate, image of physical education. As one pamphlet advertised, "America needs alert energetic women, and a major in health and physical education prepares women for teaching, recreational jobs, camp jobs as well as helping them to become community leaders, good wives, and mothers." Majors studied a variety of team and individual sports, learning to analyze form and movement, along with methods of teaching and class organization.

Karl G. Chesnutt coached and managed various sports teams at KSU after his arrival in 1943 but is perhaps best known as the coach of men's tennis from 1948 to 1967. He was held in high esteem by many student-athletes throughout his 34-year career. An athletic scholarship was established in his name in recognition of his service to the university and devotion to students.

Primarily a club team over the course of KSU history, men's soccer held varsity status from 1963 to 1980. Coached by the ubiquitous Rudy Bachna with Isam Massad as assistant coach, the team had a measure of success in the 1960s led by team MVP Moses Musonda '67 (second row, third from left), a Latin and French major from Zambia who was named to the All-Ohio second team as a defensive back in 1964.

The women's 1967–1968 intercollegiate swimming team, pictured here, completed its second undefeated season in a row, with 18 wins, and went on to compete in the National Women's Intercollegiate Swimming and Diving Competition, placing fifth overall out of 25 teams. Top performers of that season included Grace Waldie, Muriel Forrest, Janis Smith, and Jan Haltunnen.

All-American swimmer Leslie Moore '71 placed in both the 100- and 200-yard backstroke in 1969. He won six medals in those events in the MAC championships from 1967 to 1970, as well as the top spot with the 800-yard freestyle relay in 1970. Swimmers and divers achieved considerable success in the MAC in the 1970s under Frank Vicchy and Todd Boyle. Despite that, the programs ended after the 1987–1988 season due to facility issues.

The 1960s marked a high point in KSU's distance-running history with such standout All-America runners as Pierson Lorandeau (second from left), Sam Bair (third from left), and Arthur (Art) Coolidge (not pictured here). Coach Douglas Raymond (top left and at right) served as the head track and cross-country coach at KSU for 18 years (1960–1978). He guided the Flashes to two MAC track titles (1973 and 1975) and was selected as MAC Coach of the Year two times. Raymond coached the 1973 indoor track team to a second-place finish in the NCAA championships and guided 14 KSU athletes to All-America status and 29 individual MAC titles. His athletes earned All-America status 34 times, including three Olympians, Jacques Accambray, Al Schoterman, and Gerald Tinker.

Three-time All-American Pierson "Pete" Lorandeau '71 placed in the top 10 at the NCAA national cross-country championships in 1964 and 1965 and on the track in the six-mile race in 1965. He won the MAC cross-country championships in 1964. He was captain of the cross-country team both years, during the start of its most successful era.

All-American track and cross-country runner Sam Bair '69 was the first KSU miler to break the four-minute barrier. He won the MAC mile run three consecutive years (1966–1968) and captured the MAC cross-country crown in 1967. He earned a bronze medal for finishing third in the 1,500 meters at the 1967 Pan American Games in Winnipeg.

One of the top sprinters in the history of KSU track and field, Ron Hughes '66 was an All-American in the indoor 60-meter high hurdles in 1965, placing second with a time of 7.3 seconds. During his career, he broke 12 school records, including the 45-yard hurdles, 55-meter hurdles, and 330-yard hurdles.

Distance runner Arthur (Art) Coolidge III '69 earned All-America honors once in cross-country with a seventh-place finish at the 1968 national championship race and twice on the track with a fifth-place finish in the three mile and a fourth-place finish in the six mile during the 1969 NCAA track-and-field championships. He won the MAC three-mile run in 1969 and ran the KSU record in that event (13:42.4).

Janet and Rudy Bachna, shown above with the 1968 team and below in a later portrait, led the KSU gymnastics programs for 32 years, starting in 1959. Both served as Pan American team coaches, and Janet was head coach of the women's U.S. Olympic team in 1960. Both also participated as judges at numerous national and international competitions. Janet Bachna became the first female judge from the United States to serve as a finals judge in the World Gymnastics Championships in 1962. During their tenure, they led the KSU women's team to participation in 11 consecutive AIAW national championships, starting in 1968, four state championships, and four MAC championships in the 1970s and 1980s.

The Bachnas also founded Gymnastics in Motion, an annual gymnastics exhibition event that helped to raise funds for the gymnastics program while providing entertainment to the community. This popular annual event featured choreographed and competition routines and demonstrations of specific events. It was first held in 1964 and endured through the 1980s.

GYMNASTICS IN MOTION
To be held on
Friday, April 25 and
Saturday, April 26, 1964
at 7:30 in Memorial
Gymnasium, Kent
State University

Marie (Walther) Bilski starred in gymnastics at KSU from 1962 to 1966. She competed as a member of the 1964 U.S. Olympic team in Tokyo, Japan. She was one of the top gymnasts in the United States, winning several medals in the national championships from 1963 through 1965, as well as the North American all-around champion in 1964.

All-American catcher Thurman Munson '70, KSU's most famous baseball alumnus, hit .413 in 1968. Munson signed with the Yankees, earning America League Rookie of the Year honors in 1970 and MVP in 1976. Serving as captain for the Yankees, he led them to three American League pennants and two World Series. Munson's life was cut short in a plane crash near the Akron-Canton Airport in 1979.

Pitcher Steve Stone '70, paired with catcher Thurman Munson, formed one of the MAC's top all-time combinations in the late 1960s. He debuted in major-league baseball in 1971 with the San Francisco Giants. A major-league player for 11 years, he spent time in Chicago (Cubs and White Sox) and Baltimore, which he helped to win the American League pennant in 1979. He won the American League Cy Young Award in 1980.

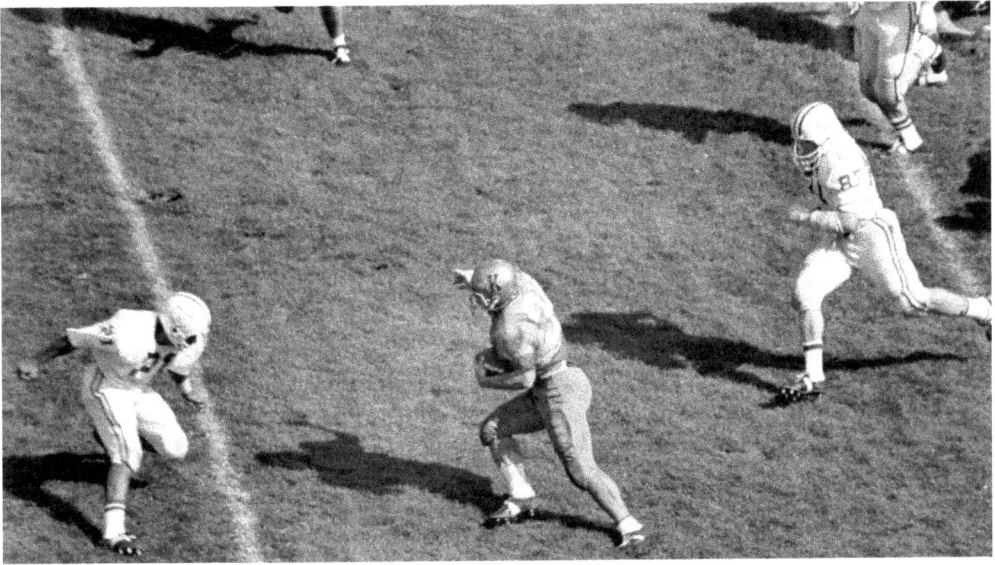

Don Nottingham (center), a 1971 marketing graduate, lettered three years in football (1968–1970), serving as captain in 1970. He was drafted to the NFL in 1971, where he played for eight years, the last six with the Miami Dolphins. KSU has recognized him through the awarding of the Don Nottingham Cup, presented annually to the top offensive player at the conclusion of spring practice.

A two-time All-MAC first-team selection (1964 and 1965), Pat Gucciardo earned honorable mention All-America recognition for his performance on the gridiron in 1965. He led the team in tackles three years and caught 13 career interceptions leading to 162 return yards. Gucciardo played for the NFL's New York Jets for one season (1966) and went on to coach the game after his playing career ended.

Honors student William (Bill) Asbury, a 1965 sociology graduate, earned three varsity letters in football and two in track as a Golden Flash. Asbury earned All-MAC first-team and MAC Offensive Player of the Year honors in 1965. He played three years in the NFL with the Pittsburgh Steelers.

Defensive back Lou Harris '70 merited All-Mid-American Conference honors as a junior and senior for the Golden Flashes on the gridiron (1965–1967). He interrupted opposing offenses with 19 career interceptions (playing in just 23 games), with a season high of 7 interceptions in 1966. Harris played for the NFL's Pittsburgh Steelers in 1968.

Don "Human Hammer" Fitzgerald set NCAA records in 1966 with 296 carries and 47 rushes in a single game. He was second in the nation with 1,245 yards in 1966. He earned All-MAC first-team honors in 1966 and 1967 and ended with 2,221 career rushing yards.

The first KSU football player to be named All-MAC three years in a row (1967–1969), Jim Corrigall later served as head KSU football coach (1994–1997). Twice selected team captain while playing for KSU, Corrigall gained the tackle record during his tenure (334). He played professionally for the Toronto Argonauts of the Canadian Football League, earning Rookie of the Year and seven times All-Pro.

A 1967 social studies graduate, Douglas Hollis Sims, a four-year letter winner in basketball for the Flashes, led the team in scoring, field-goal, and free-throw percentages and was named second-team All-MAC as a junior. Sims was drafted by the Cincinnati Royals of the NBA, one of only two basketball players from KSU to be drafted.

Best known for his incredible performance against North Carolina (ranked No. 2 in the nation at the time) Golden Flash Doug Grayson '70 hit 16 consecutive field goals and finished 18-19 and 5-5 on the free-throw stripe for 41 points. He earned All-MAC second-team honors in each of his three varsity seasons. Demonstrating his consistency, Grayson did not miss a game during his career.

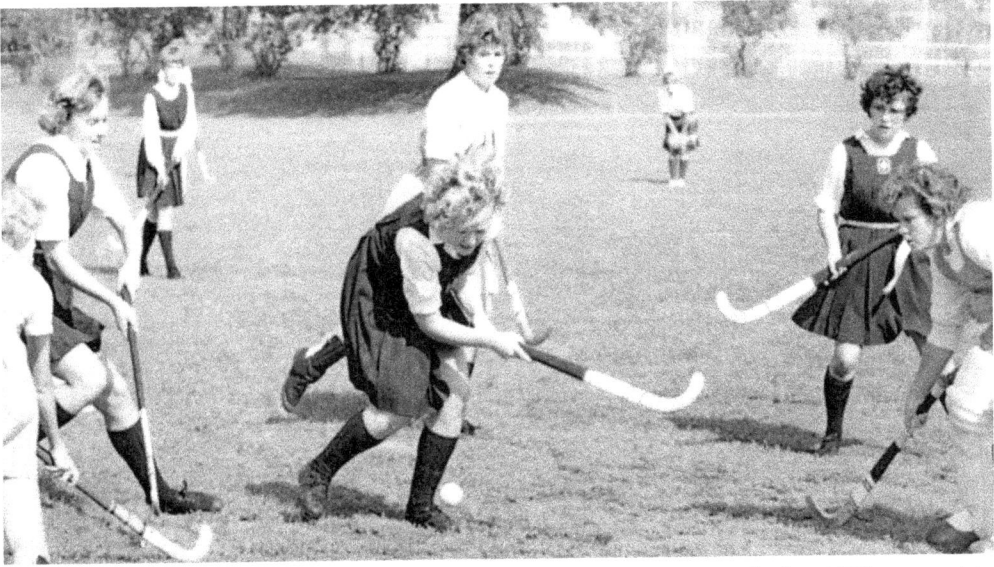

Women's field hockey, although not officially recorded as a varsity sport before 1975, engaged in intercollegiate games as early as the 1960s, and possibly well before that time. Although little documentation is to be found, yearbooks and the campus newspaper in the 1960s reported on matches with other collegiate squads. Shown here is a match with the Ohio State University in 1962.

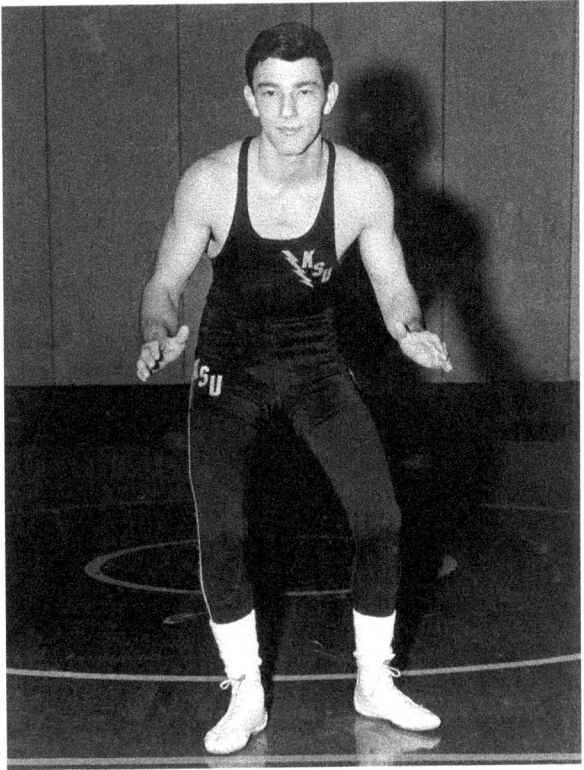

Showing the continued success of wrestling, Mike Milkovich Jr. '71 followed in the footsteps of his father, Mike Milkovich Sr., as a standout KSU athlete, going undefeated in dual meet competition for three years. Mike Milkovich Jr. earned All-America status with a sixth-place finish at 126 pounds in 1970. He was an All-MAC wrestler in 1969 (130 pounds) and 1970.

Richard "Moose" Paskert '49 (left) had a long, notable affiliation with KSU athletics as an athlete, coach, faculty member, and administrator. He started his student career in the 1940s and was a member of the noted 1946 football team. He also lettered in baseball and swimming and excelled in baseball, serving as team captain and leading hitter in 1947. After his graduation, his coaching career began and included swimming, football, and baseball. His baseball coaching career was notable for its longevity—20 years, 10 as head coach—and for the number of significant players he coached, including Thurman Munson, Steve Stone, Rich Rollins, and Gene Michael. He stepped down from coaching in 1970 and then held administrative and teaching posts until his retirement in 1981. Paskert also made significant contributions to the preservation of sports history at KSU. He was founder of the Varsity K Hall of Fame, assembled a collection of historical photographs and files, and was a walking encyclopedia of local sports history until his death in 1985.

7

The Rise of
Collegiate Sport

1970–1979

May 4, 1970, would be recorded as the most infamous date in KSU history when 13 students were shot, four of them fatally, by members of the Ohio National Guard in a clash at an antiwar rally. This event and its aftermath would intensely overshadow nearly every aspect of university life during the decade.

It is perhaps surprising that the 1970s would be recorded as one of the most outstanding periods in KSU sports history. The football program saw some of its most significant successes in the early 1970s under coach Don James and with players such as Jack Lambert (of future professional football fame), Larry Poole, Cedric Brown, Abdul Salaam (Larry Faulk), and Greg Kokal. In 1972, the players won their only MAC championship and ended the season with a Tangerine Bowl appearance. There were also a number of standout track athletes during this period, several of whom also competed in the 1972 Olympics. Men's swimming had notable achievements under coach Tod Boyle, who was named MAC Coach of the Year five times between 1973 and 1979.

The passage of national Title IX legislation in 1972, guaranteeing equal educational opportunities based on sex, signaled the start of a new era of intercollegiate athletic competition for women. However, it would not be until the 1980s that these would begin to develop into full-fledged programs.

In 1973, the NCAA reorganized into three competitive divisions, with KSU choosing to join the most competitive, Division I. This changed competition and scheduling practices and set the stage for the development of the MAC. Also, late in the decade, the intramural program at KSU would begin to flourish as it gained greater institutional support (including a larger staff), expanded facilities, and an increase in the variety and number of activities offered.

Several athletic facilities were built during the decade, including a new football stadium; an ice arena; the health, physical education, and recreation building; and the University School's Robert O. Hall Athletic Field. The decade came to a close with the razing of the original Wills Gymnasium.

Immediately following the shooting of 13 students by members of the Ohio National Guard, on May 4, 1970, the campus was ordered closed, and all students were sent home. In the weeks immediately following, faculty members were instructed to communicate with their students by mail, off-campus meetings, and other means and to find ways to allow students to complete their coursework and receive final grades for the spring quarter. Forty days after the close of campus, commencement ceremonies were held for 1,250 graduating seniors and graduate students. Days later, the university was reopened with the start of the summer quarter. In the years that followed, as the university dealt with this devastating event, athletic pride and intramural sports participation would be promoted by some as tools for rebuilding a sense of community on campus.

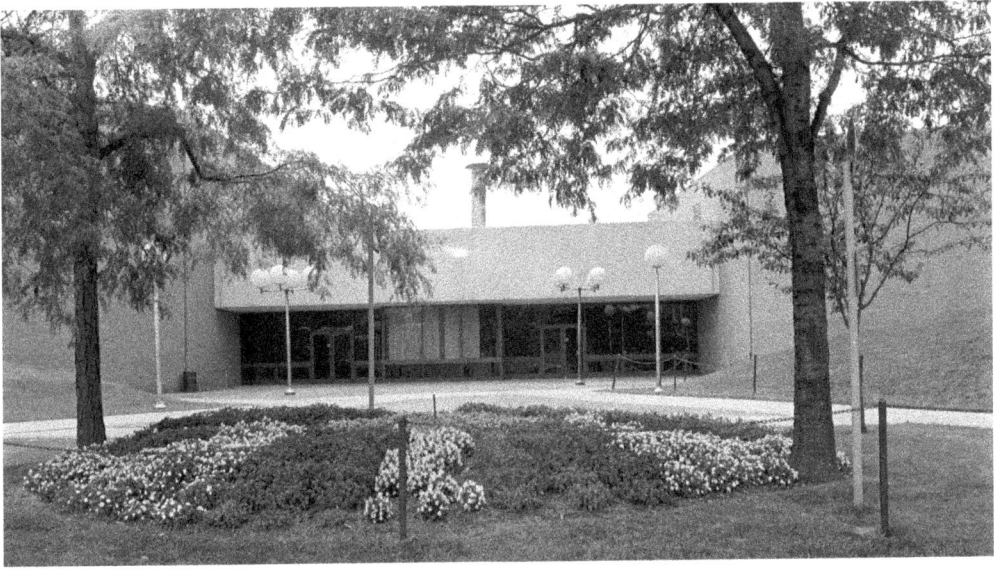

The ice arena was built in 1970 and included a hockey rink, recreational rink, and lounge area complete with a fireplace and snack bar. This facility was home to the Clippers ice hockey club and varsity hockey team, from 1980 to 1994, and also served as a recreational skating facility. Today the building is used for community skating, ice hockey instructional programs, and activities of the Kent Skating Club.

A new stadium was constructed on the far southeastern edge of campus, off Summit Street, near its intersection with Route 261. Dedicated in 1970, it became the new home of the Golden Flashes football and field hockey teams. At the time of construction, seating capacity was 30,520. In 1973, its official name was changed to Dix Stadium, in honor of longtime trustee Robert Dix.

While only at KSU a short time (1971–1974), coach Donald (Don) James led the Flashes' football program, known as the "James Gang," during its most victorious time with KSU's only MAC championship and a trip to the Tangerine Bowl in 1972. James left KSU to work as the head coach at the University of Washington, where he continued his success.

Leading KSU rusher Larry Poole, second in the nation in scoring in 1973, helped the football team create one of its strongest eras. He set many records during his time, including career yards rushing (2,668) and most touchdowns in a season (18) and career (38). The Cleveland Browns drafted him in 1975, and he later also played for the Houston Oilers.

Perhaps the most famous KSU football alum, Jack Lambert (No. 99) played a starring role on the James Gang as middle linebacker. He led the MAC with 233 tackles in 1972, earning MAC Defensive Player of the Year honors. The 1972 Tangerine Bowl MVP finished his KSU career with 593 tackles. The Pittsburgh Steelers selected him in the 1974 draft where he became part of the "Steel Curtain" defense for the next decade that helped the NFL team to four Super Bowl victories. The United Press International twice selected Lambert as the Defensive Player of the Year (1976 and 1979). Selected All-Pro eight times, Lambert played in the Pro Bowl nine times, a record for a linebacker. The Pro Football Hall of Fame inducted him in 1990.

Nick Saban '73 played defensive back for KSU in the early 1970s. He started at cornerback as a sophomore in 1970 and then at safety his last two years. He contributed to the Golden Flashes winning the 1972 MAC title, although injuries caused him to miss the last few games of the season. He started his illustrious coaching career as a KSU graduate assistant in 1973 and 1974.

Greg Kokal '80 directed the Golden Flashes to their only MAC football championship and Tangerine Bowl berth in 1972. He lettered four times (1972–1975) and was team captain as a senior. He ranked eighth in the NCAA in total offense (2,010 yards) as a senior and set the KSU record for most passing attempts in a game (42) in the Tangerine Bowl.

Gary Pinkel '75 was the leading receiver on KSU's 1972 MAC championship team, grabbing 34 passes for 477 yards and three touchdowns. He led KSU in receiving as a senior with 36 catches for 409 yards, helping the Golden Flashes post the best record in school history (9-2-0). He was named to the All-MAC first team at tight end in 1972 and 1973 and as an Associated Press honorable mention All-American in 1973.

CAPT. FLASH

December 29, 1972

in this issue...

The Tangerine Bowl Caper

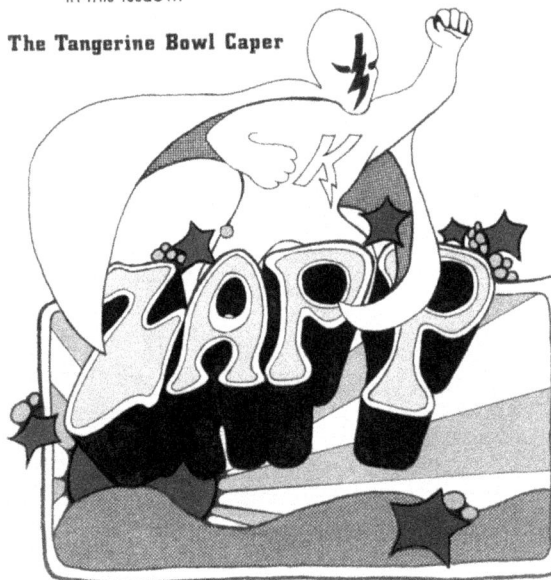

The 1972 football season unexpectedly became one of the most memorable in the sport's beleaguered history at KSU. After finishing last in their conference the previous season, the Flashes' next season ended in their defeat of Toledo University and capture of their first-ever MAC championship. The team then saw postseason action at the Tangerine Bowl on December 29, 1972, facing Tampa, which defeated them 21-18.

Defensive back Cedric Brown, another key contributor to KSU's winning ways in the 1970s, led the nation with eight interceptions in eight games as a senior in 1975. The Oakland Raiders of the NFL drafted him in 1976. He played for the Tampa Bay Buccaneers 1976–1984, where he earned team MVP honors in 1981.

Abdul Salaam '80, whose name means "soldier of peace" (Larry Faulk when he played at KSU), was twice selected to the All-MAC first team as a defensive lineman (1973 and 1974) and led his team as captain in 1975. The New York Jets of the NFL drafted Salaam, and he played with them from 1976 to 1983.

After a playing career that ended in 1978 with 645 tackles, John "Jack" Lazor (right) stayed on to serve as an assistant coach in 1979 and 1983. While playing for KSU, Lazor earned All-MAC first-team honors 1976–1978, honorable mention Associated Press All-American in 1977, and Associated Press third-team honors in 1978.

Wrestler Ron Michael '79, a 66-11-1 career grappler, twice won the MAC championships at 158 pounds. He earned All-America status with a fourth-place finish at the 1978 NCAA championships. As a senior, Michael was a recipient of the Joe Begala Award presented annually in recognition of academic achievement and wrestling skill. The award is named in honor of prestigious wrestling coach Joseph Begala.

Wrestler Steve Reedy '82 (third from right) finished his KSU athletic career with 110 wins, which included 38 dual-match victories in 1980–1981 alone. He won the MAC championship at 167 pounds, earning a trip to the NCAA championship meet in 1981, where he placed sixth and earned All-America honors. He helped lead the Flashes to a 44-12-1 dual-meet record, four MAC team titles, and two top 20 NCAA rankings under coach Ron Gray.

Triple All-MAC first-team player Burrell McGhee is shown here scoring against Big Ten cagers University of Iowa. He lit up the Memorial Gymnasium from 1977 to 1979, scoring 1,710 points over the course of his career. During the 1977–1978 season, McGhee was 12th in the nation in scoring, with an average of 21.9 points per game. McGhee's life and promising future were cut short when he was murdered in 1981.

Football player and sprinter Gerald Tinker excelled on the gridiron, on the track, and in the classroom. As well as being a member of the All-MAC academic team in 1972, he ran the third leg of the 4-by-100-meter relay team that won gold at the 1972 Olympic Games for the United States, followed by the NCAA indoor championship in the 60-meter dash in 1973. He ranked fifth in the nation as a punt return specialist while also playing wide receiver for KSU. The Atlanta Falcons picked him in the second round of the NFL draft in 1974, where he played two years, followed by a season with the Green Bay Packers.

One of the top two weight men in the country, both at KSU, Jacques Accambray '74, shown at left throwing the 35-pound weight, earned All-America status seven times in his time as a Flash (1971–1974), three in the weight throw (indoors) and four in the hammer. He won two NCAA hammer titles (1971 and 1973). With teammates Ted Harris and Gerald Tinker, he led the Flashes to second place at the 1973 NCAA indoor championships. He represented France in the 1972 Munich Olympic Games. Five-time All-American thrower Al Schoterman '73, shown below winding up to throw the hammer, faced some of his toughest competition from teammate Accambray. Schoterman won the NCAA indoor championship weight throw (1971) and the NCAA championship hammer (1972). He represented the United States at the 1972 Olympic Games.

Another on the list of outstanding weight men in KSU's history, Jud Logan '82 won the MAC championship hammer throw in 1979 and 1980 and discus throw in 1980. Logan went on to compete for the United States in four Olympic Games in 1984, 1988, 1992, and 2000. Logan, a nine-time U.S. championship or Olympic Trials gold medalist, also held the American record for the hammer at several points in his career.

Another to contribute to the second-place team finish at the 1973 NCAA indoor championship meet, middle-distance runner Ted Harris earned All-America status with his third-place finish in the 880-yard run. His effort helped KSU to its highest national finish ever in this contest. He also contributed to KSU's MAC championship that same year.

Cross-country standout Dwight Kier '75 placed second at the 1974 MAC cross-country championship as a junior, placed fifth at the NCAA regional, and was 24th among Americans at the national championships en route to All-America honors. Kier contributed to two track-and-field team MAC championship titles, in 1973 and 1975.

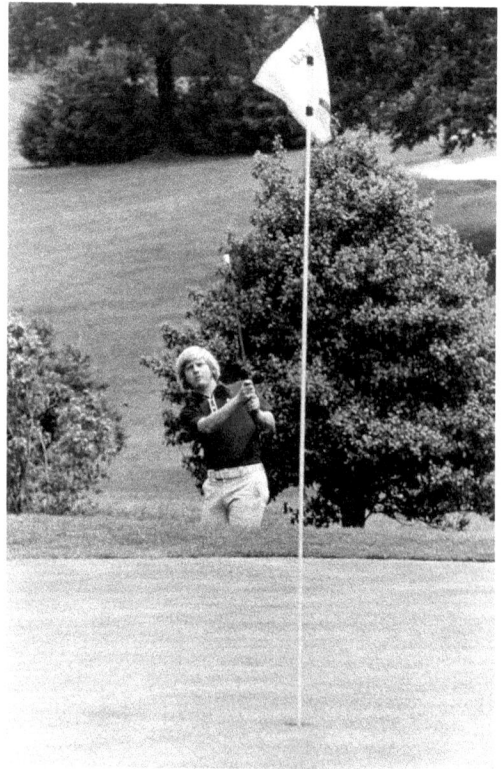

Golfer Mike Morrow, a 1975 parks and recreation management graduate, earned 1973 All-America honorable mention and All-MAC recognition three times (1972, 1973, and 1975). He played professionally from 1978 to 1991, earning 26 PGA section tournament victories. He returned to KSU in 1990 as head professional and manager of the KSU golf course. In 1997, he helped to create and has since led the tremendously successful KSU women's varsity golf team.

In 1975, Judy K. Devine became assistant athletic director, with an emphasis on administering and expanding women's intercollegiate athletics programs. A graduate of Colorado State University, she had come to KSU as a graduate student in 1969 and became a physical education professor in 1973. During her tenure, Devine also coached women's basketball and field hockey. In 1978, she was made associate athletic director. In 2000, she retired after 31 years of service.

Field hockey player Sue (Jensen) Sweeney '80 became the Golden Flashes' most prolific scorer in her four seasons at KSU, leading her team each of her last three seasons. She finished her career with a season-high record of 26 goals, with 128 for her career.

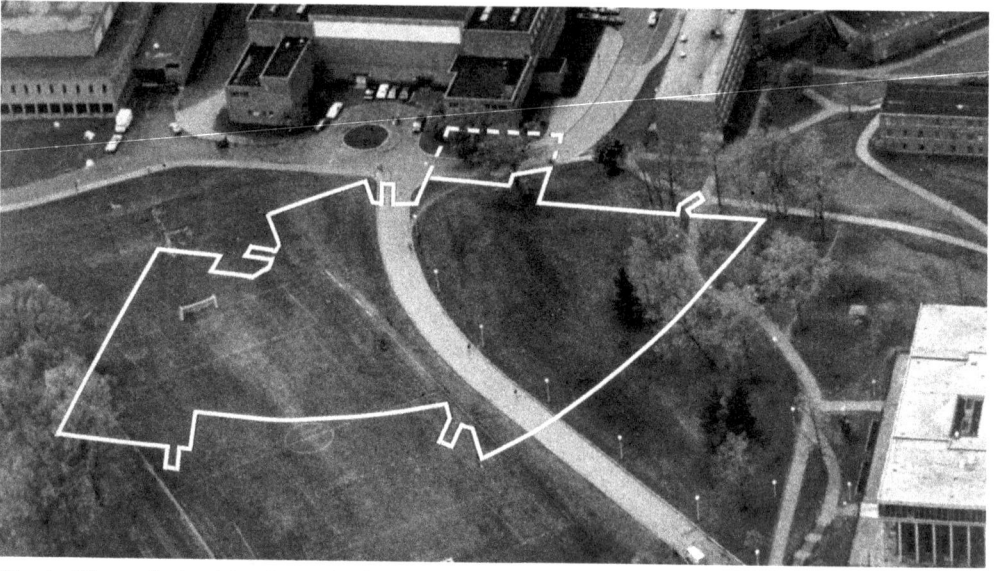

The building of a health, physical education, and recreation annex onto the existing gymnasium was steeped in controversy as the proposed building site overlapped that of the 1970 shootings. Students, alumni, and others, led by the May 4 Coalition, protested the planned annex construction, even camping out on the site in an extended protest that became known as "Tent City." Despite these efforts, attempts to stop the construction were unsuccessful.

As this architectural sketch shows, the gymnasium annex was planned to meet the multipurpose needs of physical education, recreation, and athletics. Shortly after its opening, additional facility improvements and expansions were undertaken to support an expanding intramural program, including resurfacing of tennis courts, construction of a new lighted soccer, football, and softball field, and improvement of the Allerton baseball fields.

8

BUILDING TRADITION

1980–1989

Nationally, the NCAA faced growing controversy over the role of Division I athletics in education. While the issues were not new, the scale of and attention to the commercialism of collegiate sports gained significant attention in the 1980s. Mid-major institutions such as KSU, however, remained below the radar as they continued to function as nonprofit entities. Although women's intercollegiate programs had been in place in several sports since the mid-1970s, the 1980s saw their strengthening and further development, with the takeover of women's athletics by the NCAA in 1980. Outstanding individual athletes, including Bonnie Beachy (basketball and tennis), Tami (Brown) Hartley (field hockey), and Pauline Maurice (softball), would make their mark during the decade. The women's gymnastics team continued its strong record of success with four MAC championships and four team competitions in the NCAA championships throughout the decade. Judy Devine, appointed in 1975 as assistant director of athletics, was responsible for the administration and expansion of women's intercollegiate athletics during this critical decade of development.

Following Donald Dufek's retirement, KSU alumnus and former football player Paul Amodio '55 was appointed athletic director in 1980, a post he held until 1994. Under Amodio's directorship, nearly all athletic facilities were upgraded, and the field house was constructed in 1989.

Outstanding male athletes of the decade included Thomas Jefferson (track), Randy Bockus (baseball), Ray Wagner (wrestling), Bert Weidner (football), Eric Wilkerson (football), and Rob Moss (golf). Men's gymnastics had a very strong decade with coaches Terry Nesbitt and José Velez at the helm. The wrestling program, as in almost every other time in school history, continued its success. Although "new" wrestling coach Ron Gray, appointed in 1972, had suffered four initial rough seasons, he regained the program's highly successful track record, guiding the Flashes to six consecutive MAC team championships from 1977 to 1982.

Despite the continued growth of varsity sports, student interest in intramural and club sports remained very strong throughout the decade. An amazing variety of programs were offered, including the alpine ski team, fencing, ice-skating, kayaking, wheelchair basketball, scuba, men's rugby, sailing, and martial arts, among others.

After 10 years of operation as a club sport, ice hockey was designated as an intercollegiate varsity sport in 1980, and former Olympian Doug Ross, who had coached during the previous club season, continued on as head coach of the varsity team. The sport would not enjoy a long history at KSU; it was eliminated in 1994 as part of the university's effort to contain costs associated with intercollegiate athletics.

Continuing a long thread of success, wrestler Ray Wagner '82, three-time MAC heavyweight champion (1979, 1980, and 1981), earned All-America status, placing fifth in the NCAA championship meet in 1981. Wagner also played football for the Flashes and went on to play professionally for the United States Football League's Denver Gold.

The only woman in KSU history to have her uniform number (13) retired, Bonnie Beachy '82 earned seven varsity letters, four in basketball, three in tennis, from 1979 to 1983. She became the leading all-time scorer in basketball with 2,071 points over her career. She was selected to the Kodak All-Region team as a junior and senior.

Three-time MAC 200-meter dash champion Thomas Jefferson set the conference records for the 200 (20.43) and 100 (10.25) in 1984. He captured three conference titles in the 100-meter dash (1982, 1984, and 1985) and earned Outstanding Performer recognition by the MAC twice (1984 and 1985). Jefferson won bronze for the United States at the 1984 Los Angeles Olympic Games in the 200-meter dash to complete a U.S. sweep.

In an effort to increase school spirit and enthusiasm for intercollegiate sports, the athletics department unveiled a new mascot for the Golden Flashes in a series of special homecoming events in 1985 (the university's sesquicentennial anniversary). Students in the Kent Technology Education Club (above) put in 265 hours of work to construct a giant egg out of wood, plaster, fiberglass, and resin, while Craig Hollinger (below) and other staff members of the grounds department created a natural nest in which to nestle the egg. The identity of the new mascot was kept secret leading up to homecoming weekend. The "mystery egg" then became part of a special homecoming parade float, news conference, and football game halftime spectacle.

During halftime of the homecoming game against the University of Texas at El Paso, spectators were treated to an unusual display when a live golden eagle owned and handled by Earl Shriver of Baden, Pennsylvania, soared into the stadium, followed by the appearance of the new Flash mascot. Fans also received golden tokens featuring the new KSU athletics logo—a stylized golden eagle with a lightning bolt extending from one wing superimposed over the letter K. Although met by some student scorn at the time of its unveiling, the golden eagle has endured as the school's official mascot to this day.

According to local lore, a wheel from the wagon of University of Akron founder John R. Buchtel was unearthed during a pipeline dig near the KSU campus. KSU dean of men Raymond Manchester came into possession of the wheel and suggested that this "trophy" be awarded to the victor of each KSU-Akron football game. Nearby University of Akron is a longtime rival. The wagon wheel tradition has endured since 1946.

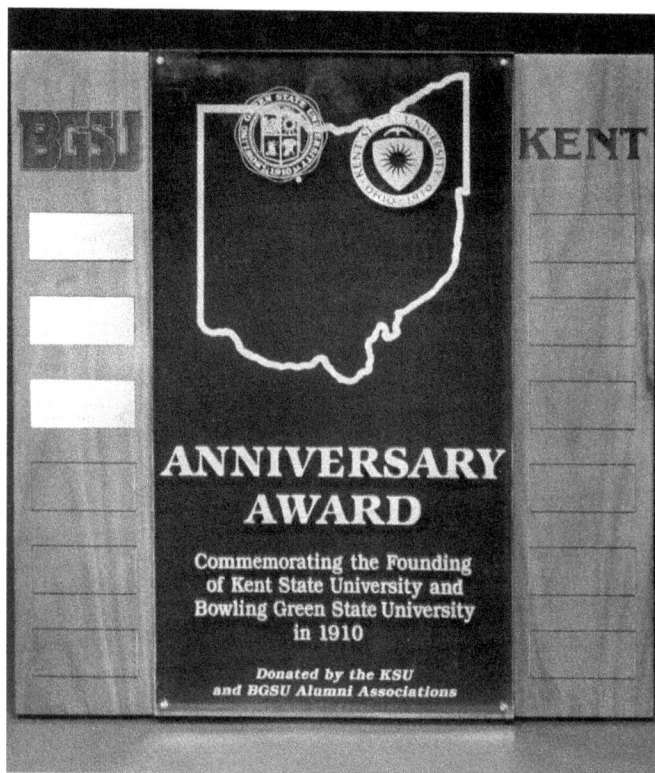

The Anniversary Award, an athletic rivalry tradition between KSU and Bowling Green State University, was established more recently. Both schools were founded in 1910 via the same piece of state legislation that created two normal schools in northern Ohio—one in the east and one in the west. The award was mutually established by each school's alumni association in 1985, the 75th anniversary of each institution.

To mark the 1988 renewal of the KSU–Youngstown State football series, Schwebel Baking Company sponsored a trophy and scholarship award that would go to the winning side of each matchup. The teams, which had last met in 1948, have since faced each other eight times in the Schwebel Challenge Series. Shown here (from left to right) in 1988 are KSU coach Richard Crum, company president Joseph Schwebel, and Youngstown coach James Tressel.

The KSU Wheelchair Athletic Club, a student organization, was founded in 1973. Members took part in a variety of athletic events and interschool competitions, including the ever-popular wheelchair basketball league. Pictured here are members of a 1980s Wheelchair Flashes basketball team. For many years, KSU has had a good reputation for the accessibility of its campus and providing meaningful support services to differently abled students.

Baseball player Randy Bockus was selected first-team All-MAC in 1981 and 1982 and a second-team pick in 1980. He led the MAC in hitting as a junior and was second in the NCAA that season with a .480 average. His career batting average of .391 broke Thurman Munson's record of .390. The San Francisco Giants drafted Bockus, and he played for several teams before his professional playing career ended in 1991.

The MAC named basketball player Judi Dum '88 (left) Freshman of the Year in 1984. She went on to become a three-time All-MAC selection (honorable mention 1983–1984, second team 1985–1986 and 1986–1987). She concluded her career at KSU with 870 rebounds and 1,648 points, landing third overall in rebounds and seventh among career scorers to date.

Kris Ewing '83 started at KSU as a member of the Golden Flash field hockey team (1980–1982). Following her playing career, she served as the assistant field hockey coach at KSU in 1984 and then continued her education by pursuing a master's degree in physical education at the University of Iowa (1985). She returned to KSU and served as head field hockey coach from 1985 to 1993.

As the top goal scorer, junior Tami (Brown) Hartley '90 led the Golden Flashes to their first field hockey MAC regular-season and tournament championship wins in 1988. Brown gained recognition as a two-time first-team All-MAC and second-team All–Midwest Region pick in the late 1980s. A four-year letter winner, she topped the team in goals and points each of her last three seasons.

Trent Grooms '80, one of the most dominant inside players in KSU hard court history, posted career numbers of 1,268 points and 1,012 rebounds. Grooms led his teams in rebounding in each of his four seasons, ranking seventh in the nation with 12.3 rebounds per game as a senior. As a Flash, he achieved 55 double-figure rebounding games and started 67 consecutive games. The NBA's Kansas City Kings drafted Grooms in 1980.

Basketball player Anthony Grier '85, a unanimous pick to the All-MAC first team, also received All-America honorable mention in the 1984–1985 season. He averaged a team-leading 20.9 points per game that season, the most by a KSU player in the previous 23 years. Under the guidance of coach Jim McDonald, he helped lead the Golden Flashes to their first postseason play with a berth in the 1985 National Invitation Tournament.

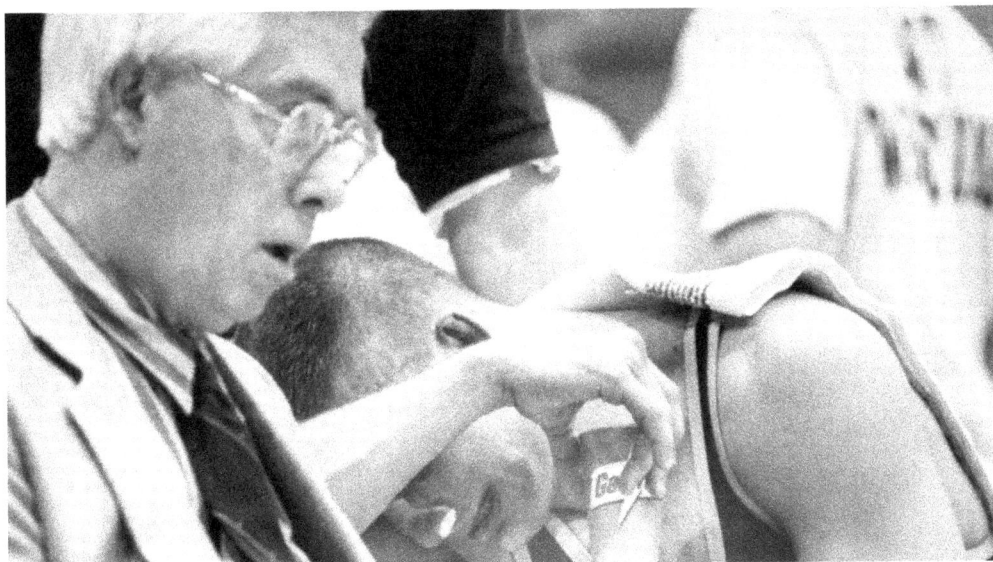

Ronald Gray (left) wrestled at Iowa State University, capturing two NCAA titles and a runner-up finish. Gray served as head coach of the Golden Flashes for 25 seasons (1972–1996). He posted a 233-112-5 mark, guiding the grapplers to nine MAC team championships. The MAC named Gray Coach of the Year five times. KSU wrestlers won 46 individual MAC titles and earned All-America accolades six times under his tutelage.

Grappler Don Horning (right) transferred to KSU after posting a 54-13 mark at Northwestern University to become KSU's first two-time All-American after finishing third in the NCAA tournament at 118 pounds as a junior in 1985 and seventh at 126 pounds as a senior. He captured the MAC championship as a junior. He posted a 46-4-1 record with 21 pins for the Flashes.

Golfer Rob Moss '90 earned three-time All-MAC first-team honors as a Flash (1988, 1989, and 1990). He was the MAC tournament medalist in 1988, and the conference named Moss Sportsman of the Year in 1990. He twice played his way onto the All-District team (1988 and 1990). The College Sports Information Directors Association Academic All-District pick (1990) was also selected as a Golf Coaches Association of America All-America Scholar-Athlete (1989 and 1990).

A field house was built in 1989 to accommodate football practice, soccer, baseball, softball, field hockey, golf, and track-and-field events. With a construction cost of $6.6 million, the facility was built adjacent to Dix Stadium and included a full-size indoor football field, a six-lane track, and training facilities.

9

WOMEN'S SPORTS

ON THE RISE

1990–1999

At KSU, the 1990s were highlighted by major development in women's athletics, excellence in several men's and women's programs, and continued improvement of facilities. Baseball saw perhaps its most successful record up to that point during the early 1990s, with four regular-season MAC titles and two MAC tournament championships. Other programs also charted great success during the decade, including softball (finishing seventh overall in the NCAA national tournament in 1990), field hockey, men's and women's basketball, and men's golf. Two new women's intercollegiate programs would also be established late in the decade—soccer in 1997 and golf in 1998.

On the national level, several developments occurred, including the 1992 *Franklin v. Gwinnet County Public Schools* Supreme Court decision, the release of the NCAA gender equity report in that same year, an increase in federal spending for the Office for Civil Rights that oversees Title IX complaints, and the 1994 Equity in Athletics Disclosure Act, all of which resulted in more meaningful, demonstrable compliance with the law. This contributed to the tremendous growth in women's athletics throughout the 1990s, which had already seen significant gains in the previous decade.

Men's gymnastics and ice hockey were eliminated in 1994, following the university's Intercollegiate Athletic Committee's extensive evaluation of the 18 intercollegiate sports programs in place at the time. With the MAC requirement to field football and NCAA requirements for football attendance, KSU faced economic pressures shared with other mid-major programs. Following this decision, the remaining 16 sports programs included nine women's and seven men's teams encompassing the following sports: baseball, basketball, cross-country, football, golf, track and field, wrestling, field hockey, gymnastics, soccer, softball, and volleyball.

In keeping with national trends toward increased spending on facilities, the Memorial Gymnasium was renovated extensively in 1992 and a new facade was added to the building. In 1999, a modern student recreation and wellness center was built and became the center of many of the intramural, club, and fitness programs formerly housed in the gymnasium and gymnasium annex.

The softball team started the decade on a high note when it ended its 1990 season with a trip to the Women's College World Series, placing seventh in this highly competitive tournament. During that memorable season, KSU posted a 43-9 overall record and a 20-4 mark in the MAC with both victory totals still standing as school records. Pictured here are team members with the MAC championship trophy.

Sue Lilley-Nevar served as head coach of the KSU softball team from 1986 to 1996 and is best remembered for directing the Golden Flashes to the 1990 Women's College World Series. A native of Fairlawn, she also holds the school's career wins record with 289. Among her players are two All-Americans, Pauline Maurice (second team) and Darby Seegrist (third team) in 1990, and nine All-MAC first-team players.

Under coach Herb Page '74, the men's golf team charted great success in the 1990s, including seven MAC championships (1992–1995 and 1997–1999) and a NCAA Central Region championship (1993). The program's excellence would continue into the 21st century. Pictured here (from left to right) are 1993 captains Ron Mamrick and Rob Wakeling, along with three-time All-American Eric Frishette. All-Americans of the 1990s included Bryan DeCorso, Kevin Kraft, and David Morland, among others.

Following in the footsteps of 1980s offensive powerhouse Eric Wilkerson, Astron Whatley '98 became a team leader in rushing in each of his four years in the football program. Whatley, who still holds the school records in career rushing attempts (878) and net yards rushing (3,989), was named MAC Freshman of the Year in 1994 and was a three-time All-MAC team selection.

No player had approached Bonnie Beachy's career scoring totals for a decade until the arrival of Tracey (Lynn) Dawson '95. She boasted a career total of 2,066 points (just five points shy of Beachy's record), ranks first overall in scoring percentage, and holds the KSU women's record for rebounds (990) to date. She was named MAC Freshman of the Year in 1991.

One of the top 10 career scorers in KSU women's basketball, Dawn Zerman '00 earned career totals of 1,685 points, 467 assists, and 320 steals. She received All-America honors along with being named MAC Freshman of the Year (1997) and MAC Player of the Year (2000), along with many other conference accolades. During her tenure, the team won three MAC season titles and two conference tournament championships and appeared in two NCAA tournaments.

Track and cross-country star Debbie Duplay-Blank '93 was the first woman in KSU history to qualify as an NCAA All-American in track. A middle-distance runner, she won the 1993 MAC championship in the 1,500 meters. She was selected for the All-MAC cross-country team in 1992 and was an All-American in the 800 meters in 1993.

Another standout runner was Jennifer Buckley '95. She is distinguished as KSU's first four-time female All-American—two times each for the indoor and outdoor 800 meters event. She was named the NCAA Ohio Woman of the Year in 1995. She was a two-time MAC champion in the 800, set both the indoor and outdoor school records in that event, and was a semifinalist at that distance in the 1996 U.S. Olympic Trials.

Three-time All-American discus and weight thrower Roberta Collins competed at the national championships in the discus each of her four years at KSU and placed fifth at nationals in 1997 (177-7). She also made a mark for herself within the MAC as an eight-time conference champion. She won the indoor weight throw four years in a row and in outdoor competitions won the shot put once and the discus three times.

The women's volleyball program began intercollegiate competition in 1975 but has yet to achieve notable team success to date. Four-year letter winner Larisa Grinbergs-Kins has the distinction of becoming the first volleyball player inducted into the KSU Varsity K Hall of Fame. She is the all-time career leader in digs (1,416) and ranks third in career kills.

The 1992 MAC champion field hockey team, shown here celebrating victory, went 16-3-1 coached by Kris Ewing. Recognizing her achievements, the MAC named Ewing Coach of the Year in 1988 and 1991. Known for her work ethic and discipline, Ewing produced 32 All-MAC players, 20 Academic All-MAC players, and 14 NCAA All–Midwest Region players. She guided the Flashes to a 98-64-8 record and led KSU to unprecedented field hockey success.

Two-time All-American Maggie (Downey) Potter '00 was an instrumental part of the field hockey success story of the late 1990s. She helped lead the team to two NCAA tournament appearances (1998 and 1999), two MAC tournament championships, and a MAC regular season championship. Downey set the KSU record for career assists and ranks second in career points.

Danny Hall (center), head coach from 1988 to 1993, joined the line of highly effective baseball coaches who mark KSU's history. His teams won two MAC regular-season and tournament championships in a row (1992 and 1993). Named 1993 NCAA Division I Coach of the Year, Hall was notable for the number of KSU players he sent to the major-league amateur draft (18). Hall left KSU to become head coach at Georgia Tech.

One of the many KSU baseball alumni to make it to the majors, pitcher Dustin Hermanson, who played for the Flashes from 1992 to 1994, was a first-round draft pick of the San Diego Padres in 1994. Hermanson was the first KSU player in history to be named to the USA baseball team in 1993. He has played for several major-league teams in his 12-year professional career.

Shelly Stambaugh '97 was the first MAC gymnast in history to score a perfect 10. She attained the score four times on vault, and she also holds the KSU record in that event. Stambaugh became the first KSU female gymnast to qualify for the NCAA championships. She competed there twice, placing 19th in the overall and 20th on the vault.

Shannon Gallagher '98 distinguished herself both in gymnastics and track and field. She helped lead women's gymnastics to three MAC team championships and was winner of a MAC balance beam title in 1994. She was the third gymnast in conference history to compete in the NCAA championships. Gallagher also excelled in track and field, winning the MAC indoor and outdoor titles for pole vault in 1998.

Gary Waters (left), head coach of men's basketball from 1996 to 2001, propelled the team into what would become an eight-year streak of success, starting with the 1998–1999 season and continuing through 2005–2006. Under his leadership, the team won MAC tournament championships in 1999 and 2001, made its first-ever NCAA tournament appearance in 1999, and garnered its first NCAA tournament win against Indiana in 2001. As head coach, Waters posted a 92-60 record. He left KSU in 2001 to serve as head coach at Rutgers University and is currently head coach at Cleveland State University. The 1998–1999 team (below) won the university's first-ever MAC tournament championship in men's basketball along with its first appearance in the NCAA tournament.

10

Challenges of

Commercialized Sport

2000–2007

While Division I NCAA athletics have continued to grapple with how best to cope with the commercial success of their popularity and the resulting professionalization of collegiate sport, KSU has attempted to maintain a balance between academic and athletic goals. Athletic director Laing Kennedy has faced the challenge of ensuring academic integrity and athletic excellence while also being charged with attaining fiscal self-sustainability, a difficult goal for mid-major programs. Meanwhile, NCAA regulations for football attendance standards mean additional resources are dedicated to the most expensive sport offered. Despite these challenges, the current decade has been characterized by continued excellence in several programs, most notably golf, gymnastics, baseball, basketball, and indoor and outdoor track and field.

The golf program carried on a strong record, begun in the late 1990s, with outstanding coaches and athletes, including Ben Curtis, Jan Dowling, and Gabby Wedding. Curtis, who played at KSU from 1997 through 2000 under the direction of longtime golf coach Herb Page, would go on to become a member of the PGA Tour and the 2003 British Open winner. The women's golf team, under coach Mike Morrow's leadership, were MAC champions from 2000 through 2005.

The men's basketball team made an Elite Eight appearance in the 2002 NCAA tournament, generating excitement for sports fans throughout northeast Ohio. Baseball, which charted eight straight 30-win seasons from 1998 to 2006, would also see several players go on to major-league play during this period. Indoor and outdoor track teams boasted several All-American athletes, including 2004 Olympian Kim Kreiner, who also holds the U.S. record in the javelin.

The story of the current decade is indicative of much of KSU's athletic history. While no single sport has consistently dominated, the institution has been able to produce an impressive number of excellent teams and individual athletes, many of whom have competed at the national and international levels. Lacking the resources of many other institutions competing at the Division I level, the university has still been able to support strong intercollegiate programs in several sports while also offering a multitude of intramural and club activities throughout the century.

Following a KSU penchant for hiring KSU alumni, Scott Stricklin '95 (above, at right in dark jacket) played for one of KSU's most successful baseball coaches, Rick Rembielak, and then followed him as coach in 2005. Stricklin has perpetuated the program's success, continuing a streak of 30-win seasons to eight in 2006. He earned MAC Coach of the Year honors in 2006, following a perfect 4-0 win in the MAC championship tournament. Four Golden Flashes were drafted into major-league baseball in 2006, including MAC Player of the Year Emmanuel Burriss, pictured below, who was also named second-team All-American.

Coached by Karen Linder since 1997, the 2006 softball squad, shown above, was the most accomplished since the early 1990s and won the MAC tournament championship for the first time in school history. The team broke 26 conference, team, and individual records led by junior pitcher Brittany Robinson, pictured at right, who set 15 records, one for her 423 strikeouts that season, earning her MAC Pitcher of the Year recognition and MAC tournament MVP. To complement Robinson's defense, the Golden Flashes batters created a record-setting offense, hammering 56 home runs in 57 games, 12 of them coming at the hands of first base player Jamie Fitzpatrick.

Coach Herb Page '74 (back, center), a Golden Flash for more than three decades, played golf, ice hockey, and football as an undergraduate, serving as the placekicker of the 1972 championship team. He went on to a professional career in golf, while also contributing to KSU's golf program, becoming men's head coach in 1979. Under Page's direction, the program has amassed an impressive record with more than 60 All-MAC and 19 All-America selections. The 2000 team, pictured here, attained the highest-ever national finish (ninth) in program history. Page's most famous protégé, Ben Curtis (below), the 2003 British Open winner of the Claret Jug first made his mark as one of KSU's highest-achieving golfers, as a three-time All-American and four-time All-MAC selection. He led four MAC championship teams and had a career stroke average of 72.23.

Since the women's golf program began in 1998, it has dominated conference competition, winning nine straight MAC championships, while also gaining regional and national recognition with 18 tournament wins, led by coach Mike Morrow (above, center). The first to qualify for the NCAA championships, the 2000–2001 team, shown here, placed 15th. Several outstanding individual golfers have contributed to this success, such as Martina Gillen, Jan Dowling (back row, second from right), Gabby Wedding, and Becky Wood. Gillen, pictured at right, earned MAC Golfer of the Year honors in 2001 and 2002, winning two MAC championship tournaments, and National Golf Coaches Association All-America honorable mention honors in 2002 by shooting a 75.53 career stroke average. She won the amateur 2003 Irish Ladies championships in summer play.

Former KSU gymnast Brice Biggin '83 has served as head coach since 1992, after serving as an assistant to the Bachnas, earning NCAA Northeast Region Coach of the Year two times (1995 and 1996), five MAC championships, and NCAA Central Region Coach of the Year in 2001. As an athlete, Biggin contributed to the success of KSU's men's gymnastic programs in the 1980s along with All-American teammate Mark Gilliam '86.

Gymnast Heather Langham won an individual MAC championship title for the Flashes on the bars in 2000. She went on to earn second-team All-America status in 2002 with a tie for 8th place in the floor exercise at the NCAA championships, where she placed 14th all around. Langham averaged 9.884 on the floor that season, winning eight floor titles in 10 meets.

In 2001, Arlette van Cleef became the first Flash to earn first-team All-America honors in field hockey, also earning All-MAC first-team recognition in 2000 and 2001. She led the 2001 team in goals, assists, and points. Van Cleef contributed to two NCAA tournament appearances during her KSU career as part of a strong contingent of hockey players from the Netherlands recruited by coach Kerry DeVries.

KSU's first All-MAC first-team selection in 2003, Jackie Pecjak '04 assisted the Flashes to their first trip to the top of the MAC, with a tie for first in the conference standings, and their first trip to the MAC tournament quarterfinals. The soccer program started in 1997 with coach Colleen Marcum. Rob Marinaro has coached the team since 2001.

Javelin thrower Kim Kreiner '00 won two MAC javelin championships and became a three-time All-American in the javelin for the Flashes. She helped lead the 2000 MAC outdoor championship team, receiving All-America honors that year as well as Academic All-MAC recognition. Kreiner went on to capture the American javelin record, earn a gold medal at the 2003 Pan American Games, and represent the United States in the 2004 Athens Olympic Games.

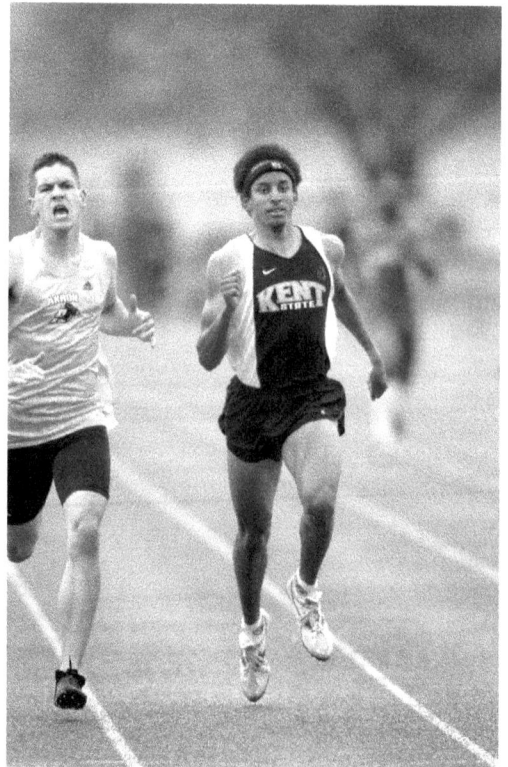

The fastest Golden Flash to date at 800 meters with a 1:47.23, a time set at the 2004 U.S. Olympic Trials, Mike Inge (right) earned All-America status at the NCAA indoor national championships in 2004 (seventh) and 2005 (fifth). Inge also won two indoor 800-meter MAC titles in 2004 and 2005 and two outdoor MAC titles in 2004, at 800 meters and 1,500 meters.

After its 2002 MAC tournament championship win, the men's basketball team earned a spot in the Elite Eight in the NCAA tournament, led by the team's four seniors shown here (above, from left to right): Andrew Mitchell '01, top scorer Trevor Huffman '02, Eric Thomas '01, and Demetric Shaw '02. One-year coach Stan Heath left the next season for the University of Arkansas. The Flashes earned trips to the tournament four times (1999, 2001, 2002, and 2006), making this one of the most successful teams on the national level for KSU. Following Heath's departure, Jim Christian (right) was named head coach and continued the program's strong track record with a career record to date of 110-51. He was named MAC Coach of the Year for the 2005–2006 season.

The KSU women's basketball team started the 21st century with a MAC championship win and a trip to the NCAA tournament in 1999–2000, repeating that feat in 2001–2002, led first by Dawn Zerman and then by Kate Miller and Andrea Csaszar, who was MAC tournament MVP in 2002. Under the direction of veteran head coach Bob Lindsay (left) and longtime associate head coach Lori Bodnar, the women's basketball program has become one of the best in its conference. During Lindsay's 18-year tenure at KSU, he garnered the most conference wins in MAC history and recorded his 300th career win in 2005. His teams have won three MAC tournaments and made 11 appearances in the MAC championship game and four in the NCAA tournament.

Coached by alumnus Jim Andrassy '94 (center) since 2003, only the fourth coach in the history of KSU wrestling, the Flashes placed second in the MAC in 2006 and sent five wrestlers to the NCAA tournament. This included the Flashes' wrestler with the most wins (126), Alex Camargo '06 (right), who won the MAC championship at 184 pounds and went on to post a 4-2 record at the NCAA tournament.

The versatile, athletic, and durable Joshua Cribbs started at quarterback for the Golden Flashes for four years (2001–2004), using his involvement in 1,755 plays to earn 18 school records. In his first year, he helped lead the team to its first winning season since 1987. He was the second player in NCAA history to have two "double-1,000" seasons with 2,424 yards in 2003 and 2,215 in 2004. He joined the NFL's Cleveland Browns in 2005.

A. O. DeWEESE   MERLE E. WAGONER   JOSEPH W. BEGALA   G. DONALD STARN

TREVOR J. REES   CARL E. ERICKSON   MILO LUDE   DONALD W. DUFEK   PAUL AMODIO

This composite photograph features athletic directors who served during the first 50 years of that position's existence at KSU. It was not until 1970 that the position was dedicated solely to administration of intercollegiate athletics. Up until that time, athletic directors had dual or triple roles, including head of health and physical education, head football coach, or head of recreation.

Since 1994, KSU's 10th and current director of athletics, Laing Kennedy, has worked to attain more national prominence and increased local enthusiasm for KSU athletics. He has brought significant facility improvements and high levels of conference success. The Reese and Jacoby Awards for top all-sports MAC standings in men's and women's sports, respectively, have been awarded to KSU three times (Reese) and five times (Jacoby) during Kennedy's tenure.

BIBLIOGRAPHY

Begala, Joseph. Papers. Kent State University Libraries.

Chesnutt, Karl. Papers. Kent State University Libraries.

Hildebrand, William H., Dean H. Keller, and Anita D. Herington. *A Book of Memories: Kent State University, 1910–1992.* Kent, OH: Kent State University Press, 1993.

Hildebrand, William H. *A History of Kent State University: Nearing a Century of Kent Pride.* Kent, OH: Kent State University, 1998.

Mechikoff, Robert A., and Steven G. Estes. *A History and Philosophy of Sport and Physical Education: From Ancient Civilizations to the Modern World.* 4th ed. New York: McGraw Hill, 2006.

Office of Sports Information. Records. Kent State University Libraries.

Rader, Benjamin G. *American Sports: From the Age of Folk Games to the Age of Televised Sports.* 4th ed. Englewood Cliffs, NJ: Prentice Hall, 1996.

Shriver, Phillip R. *The Years of Youth: Kent State University, 1910–1960.* Kent, OH: Kent State University Press, 1960.

Visit us at
arcadiapublishing.com

www.ingramcontent.com/pod-product-compliance
Lightning Source LLC
Chambersburg PA
CBHW050642110426
42813CB00007B/1889